The Truth About the Barn

Great Plains Publications
1173 Wolseley Avenue
Winnipeg, MB R3G 1H1
www.greatplains.mb.ca

Great Plains Publications gratefully acknowledges the financial support provided for its publishing program by the Government of Canada through the Canada Book Fund; the Canada Council for the Arts; the Province of Manitoba through the Book Publishing Tax Credit and the Book Publisher Marketing Assistance Program; and the Manitoba Arts Council.

Design & Typography by Relish New Brand Experience
Printed in Canada by Friesens

Library and Archives Canada Cataloguing in Publication

Title: The truth about the barn : a voyage of discovery and contemplation / David Elias.
Names: Elias, David, 1949- author.
Identifiers: Canadiana (print) 20200291815 | Canadiana (ebook) 20200291882 |
    ISBN 9781773370507 (softcover) | ISBN 9781773370514 (ebook)
Subjects: LCSH: Barns.
Classification: LCC NA8230 .E45 2020 | DDC 725/.372—dc23

Canadä

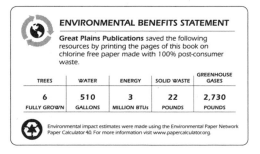

ENVIRONMENTAL BENEFITS STATEMENT

Great Plains Publications saved the following resources by printing the pages of this book on chlorine free paper made with 100% post-consumer waste.

TREES	WATER	ENERGY	SOLID WASTE	GREENHOUSE GASES
6 FULLY GROWN	510 GALLONS	3 MILLION BTUs	22 POUNDS	2,730 POUNDS

Environmental impact estimates were made using the Environmental Paper Network Paper Calculator 4.0. For more information visit www.papercalculator.org.

FSC
www.fsc.org
MIX
Paper from responsible sources
FSC® C016245

*A Voyage Of Discovery
And Contemplation*

The Truth About The Barn

David Elias

GREAT PLAINS
PUBLICATIONS

For Autrey
(Meet you at the Pony Corral)

TABLE OF CONTENTS

A photograph taken from the inside of a darkened barn interior,
looking out to the verdant countryside AUTHOR PHOTO

CHAPTER ONE

The Idea of the Barn

Through the ample open door of the peaceful country barn,
A sunlit pasture field with cattle and horses feeding,
And haze and vista, and the far horizon fading away.
WALT WHITMAN

Everything Must Go, Except ...

When Apple Corporation recently completed the construction of its new world headquarters, a stunning futuristic building in Cupertino, California, it marked the realization of a dream first envisioned by the late Steve Jobs. No expense had been spared. The price tag was a cool five billion, and the place evokes something of a gigantic circular spaceship, four stories high and almost a mile in circumference. Mr. Jobs had specified that before construction began everything on the site—old buildings, trees, asphalt—should be completely demolished and carted away, right down to the bare ground. The new facility would nestle amid an entirely re-imagined ecosystem, complete with thousands of drought-resistant trees and shrubs, and an abundance of water fountains. Everything new, everything gleaming—with one notable exception. Mr. Jobs had stipulated that one structure remain untouched. He had left strict instructions that the company should take whatever measures necessary to ensure its careful preservation.

But as planning for the construction of the new headquarters got underway, it soon became apparent that the building in question was going to be a problem. The only remedy was to take it apart, board by board, nail by nail, each item carefully numbered and labelled, and set it all aside until such time as the structure could be restored as near as possible to the place where it had originally stood. In the process, any boards that might show signs of rot or weakness would be replaced with the same kind of wood originally used in the construction.

To ensure authenticity, the trees scheduled to be taken down on the site—from which the structure had originally been built—would be milled and the planks preserved, in order to serve the needs of future restorations. The amount of effort and planning was formidable, not to mention expensive. What manner of aged, outdated building, you may rightly wonder, could possibly cause Apple Corporation to take such pains for its preservation—especially considering that absolutely everything else had to go? It was a humble barn.

It turns out the site Mr. Jobs chose for his new headquarters had at one time been part of a vibrant farming community that had almost entirely vanished, except for a single barn left standing and in remarkable condition. It had been built more than a century ago when the area bore little if any resemblance to its modern incarnation. When the incredibly high-tech building complex had at last been completed, the finishing touch required a careful and painstaking reconstruction of the unadorned barn. It stands there now, alongside one of the most sophisticated buildings ever constructed, its rough-hewn interior a place for the groundskeepers to store their equipment and supplies.

How had Mr. Jobs become so attached to it, especially considering he was not a man known to display a softer side? Those who knew him attested more to his difficult and abrasive nature than his sentimentality. It's not a unique story. A barn that has been part of someone's experience often manages to become integral to that person's life, and invariably a strong bond is formed. But what is it about these unassuming places that they should wend their way so effectively into our hearts?

The Glendenning Barn as it looked shortly after restoration
VICTOR GRIGAS/CC BY-SA

Outer Charm, Inner Bigness

There's a certain mystique about a barn that lets you experience it in ways other buildings don't allow. For me, it begins with a unique aesthetic: rough yet refined, humble yet haughty. The place has a certain smell to it. A certain sound. You can taste the inside of a barn. Allow yourself to wander through its dark and cavernous interior, run your hand along a rough-hewn timber, climb up into the hayloft, linger in the not-quite-silent gloom, and you feel yourself in the presence of a place with a soul. There's a quiet dignity about it that cultivates contemplation, renders agitation indecorous. You feel yourself getting in touch with something. You can't say just what it is, but its essence is within your grasp. Nestled in the bosom of the barn, you sense a wholesome presence, the calm reassurance of your own organic existence.

Part of has to do with all that natural wood, exposed rafters and beams lit up by a well-placed shaft of sunlight, a wagon wheel leaned against the far wall next to a few sacks of grain, a wooden ladder up along the wall, and in the alcove, a bucket hanging from a rope over the well. In the cow stall, a straw hat hangs on a peg over a pair of denim overalls, and on the rustic wooden floor, a milking stool along-side a couple of galvanized pails and some rubber boots. Through an open door, you enter a shop with old horse collars and harnesses on the wall, a workbench strewn with tools. There are shovels and axes and pitchforks leaned against the walls, a testament to the daily chores of milking and feeding and other simple labours.

Step into a barn like that and you can be transported to a place that's not so much a storehouse of hay and livestock as a repository of memory and musing. That may be something of a sentimental notion, but if you doubt the nostalgia inherent in such an idea try a little experiment. Ask someone you suspect of having a barn in their past to share a recollection, then watch as a vivid memory comes flooding back, perhaps a carefully preserved childhood reminiscence accom-panied by an elaborate anecdote that has an element of dreaminess to it. It is also possible that someone's expression might cloud over with the memory of something less agreeable or even traumatic. You never quite know what you're going to get.

Whether it's a shiny new one (rare these days) all dressed in red and trimmed with glossy white windows, or a grey and ancient relic along a country road with its weathered roof sagging gracefully, the sight of a barn catches people's attention in a way few other build-ing do. Each one seems to possess a character and charm all its own. Perhaps that's why we paint and photograph and draw them so eagerly. In many an art class the painting or sketching of a barn set against a rustic background is all but mandatory.

Mortality Close at Hand

When it comes to romanticizing the idyllic aspects of country life, what better symbol of the pastoral than a red barn with its white trim and inviting hayloft? It remains a time-honoured mainstay in books, movies, and other media, a popular setting that comes in many forms. There are sod barns, log barns, stone barns and straw barns; tobacco barns, dairy barns, and horse barns; bank barns, crib barns, round barns, and hexagonal barns. There's even something known as a housebarn, which is exactly what it sounds like. A few of them can still be found in the Mennonite villages of southern Manitoba where I grew up. Watch for them as you make your way along the solitary tree-lined street: two buildings merged into one and nestled under a common roof, usually with the house nearest to the street and the attached barn in behind. I never got to live in one myself, but I would have welcomed the chance. There was something about the idea that always appealed to me, and still does. If that sounds odd, it's only that there are a lot of barns in my past, in fact, in my youth I managed to develop a close personal relationship with a quite a number of them, mostly because I spent an inordinate amount of time there as a farm boy performing menial and often unpleasant tasks. I never imagined that in later years I'd come to think of them as places of quiet refuge and even spiritual reflection.

These days a certain element of gravitas often seems to accompany my entrance into a barn. The tides and currents of my own mortality, whose murky waters I tread awkwardly at the best of times, seem a little easier to navigate there. The atmosphere evokes something of the burial grave as I imagine it must be. It's dark. I'm surrounded by earth and wood, the musty smell of age and decay. I hear water dripping someplace. Hums and echoes filter in that seem both near and far away, the muffled movements of possible machines or animals mixed in with the strangely muted voices of people I love.

Crossing Over

In many an older barn one of the first things you come across as you enter through the wide doors is the threshing floor. You find yourself walking across a platform of heavy wooden planks laid down before you, shiny from wear, edges rounded and smoothed, softened into

The Floor, oil painting by K.B. Lebedev, 1894. Note the large wooden plank placed across the open door of the barn. WIKIMEDIA COMMONS

something abstract Dali might have painted. This is where in times past countless stalks of barley and rye and wheat, bundled into sheaves and carried in from the fields, would have been brought to be beaten with a flail by people like my grandmother and her mother before her. Here was where the precious grain was gleaned and separated from the chaff.

The straw left behind would have been pitched up into the loft above my grandmother's head, or it might have been taken outside to be burned or baled. It was the grain left on the threshing floor that mattered. Sometimes the women were so efficient in their flailing that the grain accumulated there on the floor until it threatened to spill out into the yard. But before that happened, one of the women would have taken notice and paused long enough from her labour to get hold of a sturdy plank kept on hand for just such an occasion and slide it across the doorway. Such a board would thereafter have been stepped over and referred to as the *threshold,* a term which today carries little of that original meaning.

It Starts with Colour

Ask a child to draw a barn and the result is likely to depict a building of generous size with a few windows along the side, a big set of
doors at one end, and perhaps a rounded roof with a weathervane on
top. Now ask that same child to colour in the picture and you are all
but assured which crayon they will select for the job. As refreshing
as the idea of a lemon yellow barn might be, or perhaps one that is
forest green or cornflower blue, the likelihood is practically zero. So
deeply ingrained is the idea of the red barn in our psyche that any
alternative seems all but unthinkable. It's understandable when you
consider that we hardly ever see them painted any other colour. But
how did it come to be that the owners of all those barns, from the
Alberta foothills to the North Dakota prairie to the New England
countryside, invariably felt compelled to paint them red? Was there
some subliminal proclivity in the collective unconscious of early farmers toward this particular shade?

One popular and seemingly plausible explanation holds that red
came to be the choice because farmers found it was the most effective at making their barns stand out from the surrounding landscape,
so that when it came time for the cows to find their way home from
the pasture they would have an easier time of it. The problem with
this idea is that cows, being members of the bovine family, happen
to be entirely red-green colour blind and unable to distinguish that
particular hue as anything more than another shade of grey. Another
theory proposes that early farmers, in an attempt to pass themselves
off as prosperous, painted their barns red to give them the appearance from a distance of being constructed out of brick, a building
material generally reserved for their wealthier neighbours. It has even
been suggested that the practice dates back to a time when the secret
sympathies of burgeoning twentieth-century agrarians leaned toward
communism. In fact, the reasons turn out be more geological than
political, and take us on a journey that goes all the way back to the
origins of the Earth itself.

At first glance it might seem a lighter hue would have made more sense, white for instance, which absorbs less sunlight than red and offers a stronger barrier to the effects of ultraviolet light. White also seems to be one of the few colours with any chance of passing muster as an aesthetic alternative to red. And here I feel obliged to inject a small caveat and acknowledge that there are indeed some few geographical pockets, rural Pennsylvania for one, where white barns exist, but we can consider these anomalies as exceptions that prove the rule.

To be fair, it's not as though there was an endless array of colours to choose from back then. A farmer could hardly have been expected to paint his barn Imperial Tyrian purple, for example, if only because the pigment needed to produce it can only be found in the mucus secreted by the hypobranchial gland of the Murex snail, a species indigenous to the tropics.

The reason they're red starts with the fact that early pioneer farmers were a frugal and highly practical bunch. As important as it was to protect the exposed bare wood of their newly constructed barns from the elements, it was also necessary to do so at a minimum of cost. There was little if any money to spend on extras like store-bought paint. The solution was to mix up a batch of their own, using whatever ingredients they had on hand, so long as the resulting concoction coated the wood and mitigated the general effects of weathering. The recipe they came up with (still readily available to anyone who wants to give it a try) called for skimmed milk and linseed oil to be mixed with slaked lime and red ochre. The blood from a recently slaughtered farm animal might also be added to give the hue extra vibrancy. The resulting homemade paint was easy to apply and surprisingly durable.

Red dominates barn colour for the same reason we see it so prominently in the primitive cave paintings of Lascaux, France. As pigments go, it was relatively abundant and easily obtainable to our early ancestors, who used it to render those first crude depictions of animals and birds and humans on the rock faces there. But now another question arises: why was there so much ochre lying around? Cosmologists tell us our planet was formed from the coalesced materials of an immense nebula, a vast cloud of interstellar dust. Such nebulae are not unusual in the cosmos. They are made up of material left over from the explosion of a star, and they can be found all over the galaxy. When a star explodes it's referred to as nova, or if it's really spectacular, a supernova, and when this happens the forces are so great that many new and heavier elements are created.

In case our of our particular nebula, when things cooled down the resulting cloud of dust and gas contained many of the elements that make up the earth as we know it today, including vast quantities of iron. As the solar system formed, the planets closer to the sun were left with little more than these heavier elements, while the lighter ones got blown away by the intense heat. They remained prevalent on gas planets like Saturn and Jupiter, which are much farther away. As Earth continued to evolve and water formed, oxygen became part of the equation and iron oxide was one of the compounds formed in prodigious quantities. So when early cave dwellers—and much later farmers with newly-constructed barns—were looking for a cheap and easily accessible pigment to throw into their homemade paint, there it was.

It might be tempting to make the case that a Creator, by causing the earth and the heavens to unfold in the manner just described, personally decreed it that barns should be red and that in this respect it amounts to an act of God. For my part I offer only this: that if we ever get to the point where we are able to travel to distant planets in other parts of the galaxy and discover life forms there something like ours, it seems entirely possible that some of them will have developed civilizations that construct buildings for the housing of their domesticated livestock, and that, thanks to the galactic cosmic forces I have outlined, those extraterrestrial "barns" turn out to be red.

The Star of the Show

A quick word about the ingredients for that early barn paint those farmers whipped up: the skimmed milk came from the cows they kept, of course, and the linseed oil from the crops of flax they planted. Ochre, the ingredient responsible for the giving the homemade paint its reddish hue, was derived from iron oxide, another naturally occurring and plentiful mineral which had been in use since prehistoric times. Lime was readily available (and still is) because it's among the most plentiful substances to be found naturally on the earth. However, the lime needed to be slaked, which was done by crushing the calcium oxide and heating it to yield quicklime, whose powerful "thirst" had to be quenched with water, thus yielding the finished product. Early theatrical productions employed spotlights that functioned by heating solid bars of quicklime, which caused them to emit an intense bright light. If you happened to be standing beneath it up on stage, that put you "in the limelight."

Cooking up a Batch

Homemade barn paint appears to be coming into fashion with some boutique interior designers, and numerous recipes for what is often referred to as "milk paint" are becoming increasingly prevalent. Modern-day enthusiasts extoll its use not for its economic utility but for its "authenticity." They're also eager to point out that not only is it surprisingly effective at inhibiting mold and mildew, but it's also non-toxic.

Basic Milk Paint Recipe:
In a large vat mix together the following ingredients:
- Four litres of skim milk
- Two hundred grams of hydrated lime
- One litre boiled linseed oil
- One hundred grams of salt
- Red ochre dye for colour as preferred

Apply liberally with a brush. Wait one hour between coats.

Sticking Out

The barn was almost always the largest and the most dominant building in the farmyard. In years past, a farm was deemed to be only as good as the barn that had been erected on it. Often, more attention was paid to the quality of its construction than to that of the house. In many ways it was considered more important. Without a good barn it just wasn't much of a farm. In a prairie setting such as the one I grew up in, barns dominated the landscape of any given farm. The cupola of a barn was often the first thing you'd see as you approached the yard. There might also be a silo attached to the barn. Anything that stuck out of the landscape was worthy of notice. Cities still do this by building skyscrapers. There is something about a "sticking-out-ness" that appeals to us. Perhaps it's only because as creatures we ourselves stand out because we stand up. We even train animals to go up on two legs when it's completely unnatural for them to do so. The fact that we try and get them to do it says as much about our comfort level as theirs, especially when you consider the combination of amusement and reassurance it brings us.

If They Come, You'll Build It

Before our agrarian ancestors could paint their barns, they had to build them, and here again matters of practicality played a major role in determining their structure. Every barn began with a vision, albeit a pragmatic one, an idea of what was needed to allow the daily operations of the farm to be carried out efficiently and profitably. These ideas had to take into consideration such factors as the number of cows that would need to be milked, the amount of hay that would have to be stored to feed them, allowance for other types of animal husbandry, the logistics of transport and production, etc. But all of this happened without the intervention of any formal school of barn design. "Polite" architecture had little, if any, place in the development of how the traditional barn would end up looking. Almost all architectural considerations were of the "vernacular" variety.

The basic design often fell under the mandate of a master carpenter, who hired himself out for a fee to develop an overall plan and oversee construction. The logistics of how it would go up was calculated well in advance. Trees were hewn and fashioned into timbers of designated length and size, mortices and tenons cut into place for joining. When all was ready, the able-bodied men and women of the community would show up early one morning and set themselves to the task of raising the barn.

A great many men would work in close proximity fastening anchor beams to arcade posts, securing collar ties, hammering pegs into braces, fastening rafters to ridgepoles and posts to sill plates. The women would set themselves to the preparation of food and the provision of drink. So well would everyone labour in harmony that by the time the noonday meal was ready to be served, the bones of the barn would be reaching up into the sky. Everyone would sit down at a great long table fashioned out of boards and timbers not yet needed for the raising, men and women and boys and girls taking sustenance with honest and hearty appetites the like of which shall not be seen again. Then it was back to work until the rest of the barn was up save for some roofing and siding which the resident farmer would look to on his own. By then it was evening and another great meal would be taken, often accompanied by something stronger to drink, and a celebration with music and dancing that went on well into the night.

Yes, But Is It, Well … A Barn?

Traditional barns qualify less as examples of sophisticated architecture and more as testimonials to the power of communal industry. Many are astonishing pieces of construction, magnificent in their sturdiness, each one a fitting tribute to the skills of those early builders. Function may have determined form in large measure, but these edifices have come to possess a unique character that has long made them objects of aesthetic interest, and even today they serve as consistently popular subjects for professional and amateur artists alike.

The Midway Barn on the estate of Frank Lloyd Wright in Taliesin East, Wisconsin
PHOTO WITH PERMISSION OF CARL L. THURMAN

Katharine Cotheal Budd, a pioneering architect, took the traditional features of the barn as her inspiration for the many houses, hospitals, and churches she designed. Just what that idea encompasses is open to interpretation and qualifies as a subject for discussion in a later chapter, but even some of the great architects of the world have tried their hand at designing a barn. Frank Lloyd Wright took it upon himself to build one as part of his Taliesin Estate in Wisconsin. Wright's design became known as The Midway Barn, a magnificent creation that exhibits his familiar genius of affecting an almost seamless blend of form and line (floors and walls, ceilings and roofs) into the surrounding landscape.

It's the same kind of thing he pulled off at Taliesen West in Arizona where he simply took the raw materials the desert had to offer (rock and earth and stone) and turned them into art. While his barn sets aside many of the classic accoutrements normally attributed to these structures, it nevertheless leaves no doubt as to the nature of its "barnness."

Suffice it to say that the basic essentials are all there in Wright's barn, from the quiet reassurance of containment to the courage of its simplicity. It incorporates the vernacular nature of barn architecture by paying homage to its honest character. Its stone foundation and wooden walls seek not to set themselves apart from the landscape but to complement it. The idea of the barn is thus elevated and taken to another level. More than merely respectful of the surrounding countryside, Wright's barn somehow manages to enhance it, to capture the essence of what a good barn does, which is to stand out, by necessity, but never in a pretentious manner. And yes, it's red.

Some Lofty Ideas

Most barns feature a loft, sometimes also referred to as a mow, to store hay and other fodder for the livestock. It stays nice and dry up there until such time as it's needed, at which point the farmer can simply climb up and use a pitchfork to throw some down into the mangers below. It also happens to be the most literary area of the barn. Having already left the outside world behind upon entering the barn, ascending the ladder to the loft takes you to another level. In this rarified space you find yourself elevated above the more prosaic elements below, not only in a literal but also a figurative sense. Step to the open breezeway and look out across the open countryside. You can see the big picture from up there. The world beneath is made for baser thoughts and actions, but in the loft there's room for higher levels of contemplation, perhaps even poetry.

It's where you often find things scratched into the boards or timbers, inscriptions carved by children and lovers, farmhands and fugitives. One used a pocketknife or a rusty old nail, another one an old chisel, whatever they found lying around. During the days of the Underground Railroad many a hayloft served as a popular hiding place for escaped slaves. These days it's the venue of choice in many repurposed barns, the site of countless literary readings and musical recitals, while the main floor is more likely to feature flea markets and cookie sales.

In earlier times the loose hay, and later bales, would have been carted by horse and wagon, brought in through the gable doors to be pitched up into the loft by hand, but it wasn't long before other methods were developed that didn't require such back-breaking labour. Many later barns feature a sharp triangular section of roof that juts out over the front gable, referred to as a widow's peak, where a rope and pulley hang. The pulley is attached to a railing that leads into the loft and by such means bales and bundles of hay can be hauled up into the loft for storage.

It is for purposes of storage that the roof of many a barn often slopes quite steeply up from the walls before abruptly inclining at less of an angle on up to the peak. This style is known as a gambrel roof, distinct from the kind found on most other buildings, which commonly feature a gable roof. Farmers who did the math quickly discovered that this simple alteration to the slant of the roof resulted in a significant increase in the amount of storage space for the hay they wanted to put up there. It also happened that the fodder stored up there provided good insulation from excessive heat in the summer and cold in the winter. Occasionally a barn will also have a silo attached which serves to store fermented hay, known as silage.

CHAPTER TWO

Barn as Cathedral

*Day outside finds cracks in the roof and walls of the hayloft,
and light streaks through the darkness on missions of grace and
accusation. The barn is wired to God's wrath by a lightning rod.*
VERLYN KLINKENBORG

I Will Lift Up Mine Eyes

There are certain iconic elements that immediately come to mind as
soon as the word "barn" is uttered. It starts with a set of sturdy red
wagon doors, trimmed in white and set into an expansive front gable.
As you take hold of the cast iron handle and pull, you feel the resis-
tance come thick and steady, hear the oversized hinges sigh and creak
under the weight of all that wood. The doors are split into two halves
so you leave the upper portion open, rest your elbows on the sash for
a moment and lean out into the sunshine, before turning to venture
into the gloomy yet inviting interior. The weathered floorboards creak
under your footfalls. Pigeons flutter overhead as you make your way
along the center aisle. You discover a cat curled up on the sunny ledge
of a dusty window. A sigh of wind wisps through the rafters high
above, where narrow shafts of light break in beams of shimmering
yellow. Somewhere out in the barnyard a rooster crows. You reach out
to run your hand along a hay manger where morning and evening

the cows, now out to pasture, stand to be milked and fed. The wood, shiny and dark, curves gently under your fingers, worn smooth in the most agreeable way from years of being rubbed against by those large and humble animals.

There's an aspect of quiet reverence about the place that evokes childhood memories and perhaps even a vague sense of longing. Gaze up at the rafters and you might just as well be casting your eyes into the gothic arches of a medieval cathedral. As a child growing up on the Canadian prairie, my early and artless attempts at prayer were more likely to originate not within the intimidating confines of an austere church but in the muted bowers of a lowly barn. Though the prospect of meaningful contact seemed elusive in either setting, the stall held more promise than the pew. My supplicant pleas for absolution born of transgressions real and imagined seemed somehow less contrived there and forgiveness more within reach. I was free to cast off all the bothersome trappings of culture and expectation. The barn was a private place possessed of an easy and genuine humility with little room for affectation, while church engendered pretence and ego itching to be scratched under the collar of all that piety.

From Earliest Times

My tendency to associate barns with churches may be no accident. It turns out they have more in common than I might have suspected. Consider the enormous and aged barn that sits just off the A4 superhighway emerging out of West London. With an expansive roof the colour of ochre, passengers landing at Heathrow International Airport can spot it from the air as their flight approaches the runway. This is the Harmondsworth Great Barn, a building deemed important enough by the English Heritage Society to be considered every bit as valuable as other historic sites like the Parliament Buildings or Stonehenge. It was built in the fifteenth century and even a cursory examination of its architecture reveals striking similarities to the cathedrals of that period. Indeed John Betjeman, a poet of a

Interior of the Great Harmondsworth Barn. The tall timbers and arched beams evoke a sense of standing beneath the vaulted ceiling of a cathedral.
AUTHOR SKETCH

later era who thought very highly of it, referred to it as "the cathedral of Middlesex." The resemblance is no coincidence. It turns out the carpenters of the day used many of the same techniques in its construction as they did for the cathedrals of that period, a number of which can also be found still standing in that region of England.

Enter through the gable doors of the Harmondsworth Great Barn and you find yourself under a high timbered ceiling looking down the length of a wide nave, on either side of which runs an aisle that extends to the far end of the building. It was constructed by the local parish to serve as a repository for the grain resident tenants were obliged to deliver. One tenth (thus the term "tithe") of their farm's yearly produce went to the church at harvest time and because agricultural practices were undergoing rapid improvement at the time, ever greater crop yields were making it impossible to store all of the grain coming in. The huge barn, the first of many such tithe barns, was erected to remedy the situation.

Tithe barns are sometimes also referred to as grange barns, which served a similar purpose and date even further back. They were more likely to be associated with monasteries and serve as storehouses for the food produced there. The term is derived from the Latin *granica* meaning a granary. The Coggeshall Grange Barn has a history that goes all way back to the twelfth century, a time when medieval abbeys held considerable sway over the life of the surrounding community. It is situated on the River Blackwell east of London, about a two-hour drive from the Great Harmondsworth Barn. Here Cistercian Monks farmed vast tracts of land known as monastic granges. That building had been allowed to fall into a state of terrible disrepair, but it has recently been fully and painstakingly restored. No longer used for grain storage, however, it now serves as a venue for country fairs, theatrical productions, and arts and craft sales. This has been the fate of many historically important barns in the twenty-first century, both in Europe and here in North America.

In a Stable Born

The link between barn and the Bible is hardly new, and we need look no further than the story of Jesus' birth, which saw him born in a stable. The first lungful of air the tiny Christ child took in must have carried with it the bouquet of sheep and cattle manure, and hay. Surely the heavenly father would not have chosen such a venue for the birth of his only begotten son unless he held barns in high esteem, although Mary could hardly have been blamed for wishing he might have provided something a little more amenable to her earthly needs. Talk about a lack of privacy. But then it's not the first time The Almighty insisted on making a point at the expense of comfort and decorum.

Noah's ark, too, was really nothing more than a great big floating barn—and a housebarn at that—which saw Noah and his family bed down with the livestock. Most people of European descent don't have to go all that far back in their own ancestry to confirm this same practice. In my case, a few of the housebarns built by my Mennonite forefathers are still standing and you can visit them at a historical site in a village called Neubergthal in southern Manitoba.

Church Steeple or Barn Cupola?

The layouts of early barns and churches bear a remarkable resemblance to each other, but the similarities don't end there. The cupola that adorns the roof of many a stately barn, with its ornate design and finely crafted assembly, might easily be mistaken for a church steeple. Squared on four sides, with louvres or windows and a peaked cap, the two have much in common when it comes to their construction. There's no question a cupola up on the roof lends a pleasing appearance to the look of any barn, especially with a spiffy weathervane to top it off. As for the steeple, any self-respecting church could hardly be considered complete without one. But surely they are there for entirely different reasons.

When it comes to barn cupolas, aesthetic considerations don't really enter into the equation. A barn of any appreciable size needs one as a matter of practicality. Hay breeds heat, and when it's stored in the loft of a barn for any length of time, the temperature in the interior of the stack can build up to the point where spontaneous combustion becomes a real threat. The cupola's design, with its bevelled louvres on all four sides to catch the breeze, serves to vent all that accumulated hot air out into the atmosphere. A church steeple, too, can be of use and often serves to house the church bells that summon the local parishioners to worship. If it is the job of the cupolas to disperse, perhaps it is the job of the church steeple to gather, although I like to think it plays the symbolic role as well, of venting the prayers and devotions of the congregation down below up to heaven.

Any Way the Wind Blows

It's not uncommon for both barn cupolas and church steeples to be topped off with a weathervane. Cupolas may feature a metallic rooster or perhaps some other farm animal perched atop an arrow to indicate wind direction. Pigs are popular, followed closely by cows and horses. Roosters seem to be a favorite perhaps because of their shape, with a flared tail to catch the breeze. More adventurous weathervanes sport hummingbirds, monkeys, grasshoppers, rabbits, and even crustaceans. You may also encounter dragons, dinosaurs, and squid. There's a weathervane out there to illustrate every breed dog you can think of, every mode of transportation from locomotive to tractor to motorcycle and bus, and also quite a number that depict people in various forms of engagement, such as landing a fish, for instance, or playing golf or rowing a boat. When it comes to that kind of activity it always seems to be a male. Females are more likely to be seen posing as witches or mermaids, testament to the gender gaps that lie waiting to be discovered in the unlikeliest of places.

Chanticleer

The similarities between church steeples and barn cupolas can be so striking that if only the roofline is visible you may be hard pressed to tell which is which. Church steeples are likely to be topped off with a cross but often, just like barns, feature a weathervane, and once again the rooster is popular. It may have something to do with the fact that it is the emblem of St. Peter, who heard the cock crow three times in the Passion narrative. Occasionally a church weathervane will feature a fish, which seems an entirely appropriate and perhaps even superior option. Jesus proposed to make his apostles fishers of men, after all, and upon his resurrection was offered a meal of grilled fish. Throw in all that business with the loaves and the fishes and there's a strong case to be made.

Do You Take This Barn?

It may be that the resemblance of the barn to the church has something to do with the growing trend for hip urban couples to want to get married in them. Today's prospective bride leafing through a

This country barn has been faithfully preserved by the owners, and is pictured decorated for a family wedding. COURTESY BRUCE EASON

wedding magazine or browsing online soon encounters ads that promote the appeal of "the perfect barn wedding," or perhaps "a rustic chic farm wedding," or possibly even "basking in barnyard bliss." The headlines in gossip tabloids boast of celebrities such as Kate Bosworth and Michael Polish, or Blake Lively and Ryan Reynolds enjoying their "Glamorous Outdoor Barn Wedding."

Many enterprising owners now offer their barns for rent as wedding venues and give them names like Happy Ever After Barn, The Rustic Wedding Barn, The Pioneer Wedding Barn, and so on. There are ads for the Gratitude & Grace wedding barn, Burlap and Beams, and a Touch of Country. For those couples who want something with a little more of an edge, how about getting married in a barn named Troll Haven or even Bates Barn? Wedding planners can order their personalized printed invitations from www.moo.com.

Naturally these places have been thoroughly sanitized, and great pains have been taken to banish every last morsel of manure from the site, the entire interior sandblasted, the outside painted, door handles and hinges polished, windows upgraded. In some of them the panes have been replaced with stained glass for added effect and a more ecclesiastical atmosphere. Trust me, if you haven't already had the pleasure of attending a barn wedding, there's likely one in your future.

Other grand old barns have been converted into tourist attractions, weekend getaways, or venues for displays of arts and crafts and antique road shows. The barn appears to be making something of a comeback in other areas of popular culture as well, with new ideas popping up all the time, including some that have been adapted to serve as bars, funeral homes, brothels, you name it. As with wedding barns, these places tend to have catchy names, which may account for one repurposed barn that touts itself as the perfect place to hold your "barn mitzvah."

The Nose Knows

One of the strongest elements of the barn experience is the aroma familiar to it. And this is also true for many churches, in particular those that burn incense. Cow dung is in fact an ingredient used in the manufacture of some types of incense, the smell of which always makes me feel somehow purified. I think maybe I experience something similar from the oddly pleasant smell of manure. The nostalgic and comforting smell of the barn can be really powerful. One member of the Krupp family of industrialists in pre-World War Two Germany found the aroma of horse manure so invigorating that he had it piped into his office from the nearby stables so that he could enjoy it while overseeing the sprawling factory workers below who were busy assembling the weapons that would arm the Third Reich.

CHAPTER THREE

There's No Place Like Barn

*Cosmic upheaval is not so moving as a little child pondering
the death of a sparrow in the corner of a barn.*
THOMAS SAVAGE

Creature Comforts

In many ways the essential nature of the barn rests in sanctuary.
At its heart it's a place of refuge, a haven of shelter for the humble
animals that call it home. Built for the husbandry of domesticated
creatures such as cows and pigs, it has also come to serve the needs
of pigeons and birds and mice. All animals, wild and domesticated,
want to have a home of some sort, a place they feel safe. Those out in
the wild fashion something out of twigs or straw or leaves, burrow
into the sand or soil. The place they call home may be a den, lair,
nest, burrow, warren, hive, lodge, web, cave, or just a mound. But for
barnyard animals it is the barn with all its corollaries from coop to
pen, corral to stable, sty to stall. Pets are another category altogether,
with places like kennels, tanks, and cages.

The fact of the matter is that the traditional barn still seen here and
there across the countryside is less likely to be a working barn than a
relic, preserved for sentimental purposes and little else. The modern
"barns" designed for housing large numbers of domestic animals today

This horse has a cozy little barn to shelter it from winter storms
and cold weather. COURTESY GREGG SHILLIDAY

are more likely to resemble a plant or a factory. Whether it be chickens for slaughter or egg production, cows for milk or beef, it's almost
certain to be a huge edifice that contains thousands of animals. They
may be commonplace now, but it wasn't always so, and my father was
one of the first to initiate the change.

Go Big or Go Home

The truth is that the kind of barn I've been waxing on about had a
limited place in my childhood experience. On the farm where I grew
up it was never something I could lay much claim to. As much as
I wanted it to be part of my life, my father had other ideas. By the
time I was old enough to wander about in the yard and explore the
buildings for myself, my father had decided that he wasn't interested
in such a small-time operation. The red barn was still there and my
older brother and sister assured me that there had indeed been the
usual sorts of things going on there: hay in the loft and cows in the

mangers, some pigs in a pen attached to one side, chickens squawking and pecking in the yard, the usual scene. But that was all gone now. I'd just missed it by a year or so.

By the time I wandered into to the barn I found it largely empty. Not a pig or a chicken or a horse to be seen anywhere, the concrete floor swept clean, no sign of manure, not a stick of straw. The place had been converted into a granary, just as an older barn across the yard had been turned into a machine shed by then. Long steel rods had been fixed to the walls a few feet up from the concrete, fastened with large washers and bolts on the outside to prevent the sides from bowing out and caving in under the weight of all the grain that was going to be stored where the cows used to be.

About all I could do was to wander over to my friend Delbert's place down the road a piece, where the barn with its wooden floors and stalls still smelled of bales and manure and the organic aroma of the animals. Even the light was different there. In our empty barn with its doors and windows wide open, the harsh sunlight bounced up off the polished cement. To me, it seemed a place without a soul, robbed of its "barnness."

I was left with the stories my mother liked to tell about how she used to milk cows by hand inside that barn, or sometimes just outside it. I have an old faded picture of her seated on a milk stool next to a white cow with her hands wrapped around its udders, her face in profile for the photographer. She is unaccountably dressed in her Sunday best, curly hair shining in the sunlight. Everything about that scene is utterly beautiful to me. I wasn't even born yet, but I imagine myself standing next to her, also in my Sunday clothes, watching as she milks the cow.

The idea my father had was to do things on a much larger scale. He'd gone ahead and built a barn that would hold not just a few animals, but enough to fill Noah's ark—with one important difference. Instead of thousands of creatures made up of only two of each kind, it would hold vast numbers of only one species: the turkey. He was putting up a barn with ark-like dimensions and by the time it was

My mother as a young woman, milking the cow in her heels
COURTESY KATE ROBINSON

finished, it even bore something of a resemblance to that Biblical edifice. Almost three hundred feet long, as wide as a football field, it dominated the landscape and dwarfed everything around it.

Nothing quaint or sentimental about it, no gambrel roof, no hayloft, its features were entirely unremarkable but for one thing: its size. To experience the interior of this "barn" was to enter a dark and cavernous world unto itself. It had all the charm of an aircraft carrier. But it could hold thirty thousand turkeys, and my father's dream of doing things on a big scale became reality. Things went along pretty well for a while, but by the time I was old enough to handle the tools and machinery that allowed me to do my share of the work, things had taken a nasty turn.

The problem turned out to be one of scale. In much the same way Emperor Joseph II took exception to a befuddled young Mozart's latest composition and complained that there simply too many notes, so the neighbouring farmers, still practising animal husbandry in the old humble manner, increasingly held the conviction that my father's barn exceeded tolerable limits, and further, that it involved orders of magnitude both unfamiliar and unwelcome. In short, it was just too damn big. By then I'd spent enough time observing my father to understand that it needed to be that big to stand any chance of measuring up to his ambition, but the proportions and dimensions he'd come up with constituted an affront to the community and exceeded the bounds of acceptability.

It wasn't long before some of the neighbours became distant, others vaguely hostile, not only toward my father but toward the rest of us. We heard things at school, whispers and sometimes audible utterances in places like the general store we liked to walk to on a Saturday evening for a Pepsi and a Revel. Friends repeated things to me they'd heard the grown-ups say about what my father was up to, and none of it was very nice. The pressure was relentless until it got to the point where my father, rather than admit defeat, decided instead to move the entire operation elsewhere.

A relatively insulated folk society determined to make life unbearable for one of its dissenters is not an easy thing to reckon with. An astonishing degree of crushing cruelty can be accomplished by means of little more than a subtle yet toxic mix of innuendo and gossip, so that hardly an utterance of actual verbal abuse need take place. I carried the adolescent implications of all this with me up onto the roof of the enormous barn that summer, crouched on the slanted boards as I laboured to remove the nails that held them in place. Each side resembled a gently sloping football field, and even the colour matched, as the heavy four-by-eight sheets of overlapping plywood had been treated with creosote preservative that tinted them a feral green. My father had decided we were going to dismantle the entire barn, board by board, nail by nail, and haul everything out to a parcel of marginal land on the edge of the Canadian Shield in eastern Manitoba.

The shabby house there would be a terrible disappointment and the surrounding countryside mostly bush and poor farmland riddled with fieldstones. My dispirited and compromised mother would soon discover that she couldn't even grow a decent garden. I understood why we needed to get out of the old place but when I saw what the new place did to my mother it was hard to reconcile.

I was part of a crew that included my older brother, my grandfather, and a strapping young lad named Dickie, who'd seen what we were up to from his farm in the Pembina Hills and wandered down to hire himself out to my father. Recently, my sister and I got to talking about that summer, and only then did I learn she'd harbored a secret crush on Dickie, furtively watched with secret longing as he executed cat-like maneuvers up on the roof of the barn.

My father wasn't up on the roof to help with any of the nail pulling and board lifting and timber heaving and stud hauling required for the success of the barn-moving operation. That wasn't his style. He was more of an idea man. I have a lot of memories of him giving orders and, because I still wanted to please him, doing my best to obey them. In this case that meant extracting the nails that had been driven through the four-by-eight sheets of creosote plywood and into the studs beneath. The idea was to get hold of an individual nail, yank it out without ripping up the surrounding wood too badly, and deposit it into a nearby pail for reuse at the other end of the project. To accomplish the task, I'd been issued a heavy-duty nail puller fashioned out of forged alloy steel. It featured a heavy plunger along the shaft and a tempered jaw at the tip that ensnared the head of a nail in much the same way an eagle's beak hooks into the flesh of its prey.

The exertion required to operate the nail puller for the extraction of even a single nail was formidable, but even as I worked hour after hour and day after day up on the roof of the barn I remained blissfully ignorant of the fact that this was going to be the easy part. It was the nails driven into the studs along the walls that were going to kill me. My difficulties were further exacerbated by the fact that my father had chosen three-and-a-half inch common nails to fasten down the four-by-eight sheets of plywood, a classic case of overkill meant to keep them from popping out when the ravages of repeated Canadian Prairie winters took their toll. They were never intended to be removed, and thanks to the excellent preservative qualities of all that toxic (and possibly carcinogenic) creosote, each and every one of them stubbornly resisted my attempts.

I would position the puller carefully, pound the plunger down along the shaft and sink the jaws into the wood to get a good grip on the head of the nail. Then I'd set myself and pivot, using the heel of the puller as a fulcrum to yank it up out of the wood. It rarely came out on the first try and usually required a second or third application. It was grunt work, loud and awkward and hard on the hands, and even wearing thick gloves I gave myself many blood blisters. But I kept at it. I've already told you why.

Once I'd extracted all the nails a couple of us would lift the board off and carry it away. When these had been removed, we started on the rafters and after that the studs, of which there were hundreds, and lastly the larger framing and oak timbers that held everything up. Everything was numbered and labelled before we loaded onto a fleet of trucks and trailers and hauled it to the new acreage. There everything was laid out and hammered back together again with the nails we'd saved in the buckets, and we got it all done before the snow arrived.

Years later I came across Paul Theroux's *The Mosquito Coast* and as I read the novel, I realized that with only minor changes in plot and setting that book could have written about my father. When the movie came out I sat through it, watching as Harrison Ford stubbornly carried out his wild schemes at the expense of his family, uttering his outrageous philosophies, all the while putting his wife and children through great trials that left them exasperated and yet finally somehow full of grudging admiration. One of the big questions I still wrestle with today is to what extent my father, and the rest of us by proxy, lived out the dubious moral of Theroux's tale: that it doesn't matter where you go, the world in all its petty nastiness will catch up with you sooner or later.

That spring my father resumed his turkey operation on the scale he had always intended. The barn sat in the middle of a spacious clearing around which a sturdy wire fence had been erected to keep the birds from wandering off into the surrounding wilderness, as well as prevent an increasingly plentiful assortment of predatory animals from getting at them. That was more than half a century ago, and in all that time the creosote has done its job. To this day the barn still stands where we put it up that summer. You can see it for yourself by driving out into the countryside north and east of Winnipeg, Manitoba, or you can find it on Google Earth at these coordinates: 50° 07' 49.64" N, 96° 35' 45.75" W. If you notice a large number of trees growing in the vicinity of the barn it's because the place has been turned into a charming Christmas tree farm by the latest owners. Christmas? Turkeys? The irony is almost too precious. The coniferous trees have grown extremely well there thanks to all the composted bird droppings that have accumulated in the sandy soil. The barn features a warming lounge, a tree storage area, a cutting floor, Santa's workshop and other displays for the kids, as well as deeper and more cavernous complexes of rooms and sheds.

Out of the Wild

If barns have developed into incarnations of themselves hardly recognizable to their early predecessors, the same can also be said for the animals that inhabit them. The domestic animals so familiar to the barnyard all trace their origins back to a "wild" version from which they were originally bred. The various breeds of cows, for example, whether Charolaise or Holstein, Angus or Hereford, are all descended from a single herd of wild oxen that roamed across Europe and Asia about ten thousand years ago. Sheep can trace their bloodlines back to the mouflon, an animal that resembles a spiral-horned mountain goat and is still around today. The chicken arrived at its present form by way of a particular species of jungle fowl native to Southeast Asia. And if we want to go farther back there's increasing scientific evidence that poultry in general—whether swan, goose, turkey or duck—descended from various types of dinosaurs. Recent studies by palaeontologists indicate that it was likely none other than the fearsome Tyrannosaurus Rex that evolved into the modern-day chicken.

The fact of the matter is that the barnyard animals we have become so familiar with today are among a very select group of creatures. Most animals simply cannot be domesticated. The vast majority have persistently defied repeated attempts at animal husbandry. And even where we have succeeded, underneath their tamed and seemingly docile exterior, these animals carry with them the wild instinct of the creatures they are descended from. Wolves provide us with a good example of this. Wolves and domestic dogs split from their common ancestor about thirty-four thousand years ago, but even today their genetic makeup remains all but identical. A Yorkshire terrier shares 99 percent of its DNA with a timber wolf. This may explain why you can raise a newborn wolf exactly as you would a puppy and get two very different results. At a certain point in its maturity, the wolf will suddenly and unaccountably refuse to continue behaving like a house pet.

The Salt of the Earth

If a household runs better when it's stocked with the daily necessities of life, much the same can be said for the barn. Some of us can hardly imagine a day going by when we haven't ingested something that needed a sprinkling of salt to make it taste better, and although barnyard animals have no means to make use of a salt shaker, they have no less a need for its nutritional properties. Ingesting salt by one means or another is essential for over two hundred species of mammals. In the wilderness some of them find it in the root wads of fallen trees. Moose are particularly good at this. Elephant populations in some parts of Africa are known to frequent caves where they mine and ingest rocks rich in salt content.

Animals in the wild also get it by lapping up clay deposits or licking away at mineral outcroppings or simply eating dirt. There are also places where salt is found in depressions on the forest floor, and Indigenous peoples have long known the whereabouts of these naturally occurring salt licks and congregate there to hunt for game. Some have even been given names, such as the "Blue Lick" in central Kentucky and the "Goat Lick" at Athabasca Falls in the Canadian Rockies. One resort in Africa has purposely built its hotel rooms on pillars over such a depression so that guests can sit on their balconies and watch as the elephants come in at sunset to lick up the deposits below. Sometimes animals gather at the sides of roads that have been recently salted to lick up the deposits there, an unfortunate cause of many wildlife fatalities. Hunters sometimes put out commercial salt licks in the forest and then wait for wild animals to come around so they can pick them off.

I Got a Hankerin' for Some Gravel

When it comes to the dietary needs of barnyard animals, salt is not the only mineral that needs to be supplied. Another one is crushed rock for the poultry. Turkeys and chickens and geese ingest it to pulverize the grain they eat. They have a special organ that's part of their digestive system known as a gizzard. Many wild birds also have one, which is why you sometimes see them hanging around at the side of the road, pecking away at the ground. They are picking up small bits of gravel, known as roughage, to put into their gizzards.

Free-range turkeys can usually find enough grit on their own, but it's often added as a supplement and mixed in with their feed. Some farms have galvanized steel hoppers where the birds can self-feed as much of the grit as they need. It's a cost-saving measure because the birds are more efficient at digesting their food, which lowers operating costs.

The gizzard is part of the collective set of organs sometimes used in cooking that are referred to as giblets. They are chopped up and incorporated into the stuffing, while in other kitchens they are used to make giblet gravy. The neck can go in there, too, but I consider it a delicacy and have on more than one occasion horrified my in-laws by openly stating, much like Cousin Eddie to Clark Griswold in *Christmas Vacation*, that the server should, "Save the neck for me."

A package of giblets can include the liver, but it has such a power-ful taste that it's usually prepared in a separate recipe. Pickled turkey gizzards are a popular item in parts of the American Midwest, and you can also get deep-fried gizzard in places like Chicago, where it comes with French fries and sauce. Most of the time the gizzard ends up in your pet's dried food.

The gizzard is sometimes referred to as a gastric mill, which is precisely what it is. It might also be thought of as a specialized stom-ach. It uses pieces of rock and gravel to grind up material inside the organ—a way to compensate for a lack of teeth and the inability to chew. Made out of dense muscle cells that form a thick wall, it's fairly tough eating. Back on the turkey farm there were often dead birds to eat (collateral damage) and in tough times, if you were still hungry, you took to wolfing down the gizzard.

Birds also have a crop, a sort of holding pouch situated along the neck (or gullet), where they can store a quantity of food for later digestion—kind of a variation on the cow regurgitating its food and chewing its cud. It's also known as a craw, and thus the saying popu-lar in old westerns, "sticks in my craw." As a matter of interest, the chicken and the turkey both have a crop, but the goose does not, a fact which apparently escaped Sir Arthur Conan Doyle in his writing of the Sherlock Holmes story "The Adventure of the Blue Carbuncle," in which a stolen gem has supposedly been hidden in the crop of a goose. Oops.

In terms of evolution, the crop is thought to have developed as a safety feature, because in a situation where an animal is exposed to predators while it is feeding, it allows the animal to ingest a large quantity of food quickly and then retreat to a place of safety for the process of digestion. If that bird happens to be raising a brood, this is also the place where it will regurgitate food from to feed its young by depositing it into their gaping beaks. Dinosaurs had them, too, and of course that's entirely reasonable since they are the ancestors of modern birds. We know they had them because we have found the contents, referred to as gizzard stones or gastroliths. Crocodiles and alligators eat rocks as well, not only to aid in digestion (considering they often swallow their prey whole) but also for ballast.

Don't Eat That! On Second Thought …

The ingestion of dirt may have beneficial effects for humans. Eating dirt as a treatment for gut ailments goes back to ancient Mesopotamia. Some Indigenous populations have a history of using it in some of their cooking, for example, mixing a little clay in with their potatoes or acorns to counteract the caustic flavour. A craving for dirt is still considered a sign of pregnancy in some societies, and in some cultures women will ingest clay as a way to combat morning sickness. Some of the ingredients in Kaopectate, a popular treatment for diarrhea, are derived from kaolin, a clay mineral. When humans eat inordinate amounts of dirt the practice is considered aberrant, in which case it is goes by the scientific name of *geophagia*.

Here in North America, ingesting soil as a form of introducing anti-toxins into the gut is gaining scientific credence. Some studies suggest the relatively antiseptic environment of young children today prevents them from developing a strong immune system because they lack exposure to naturally occurring substances found in the soil, which contains vital minerals and anti-toxins.

All in Good Time

Cows and other ruminants don't have an easy time of it either. The cellulose found in grass is practically impossible to digest. It's actually a lot more useful for making cardboard and wallpaper paste, also textile products like cotton fibre and rayon. When humans eat it, it pretty much goes out the way it went in, but cows have an elaborate system of digestion that makes use of four stomachs and takes a more drawn-out approach to the processing of their fodder. It requires the regurgitation of partially digested grass in order to chew it a second time before swallowing it back down again. It's sometimes referred to as chewing their cud, and if you sidle your way up to a herd of relaxed and recently fed cows lying lazily under some shady trees after a long session of grazing, you can hear them as they regurgitate their fodder with a deep gurgle, followed by the soft grinding of their large molars as they chew it again, and finally a satisfying guttural finale as they swallow it back down.

Such a Boar

The dietary preferences of barnyard animals can take some surprising turns and show up in the unlikeliest of places. I have the photographs to prove it. On a recent visit to a gated community near Phoenix, Arizona, I was warned about feral pigs that roamed the grounds at night, looking for their favorite delicacy. I thought I was being played for a northern bumpkin until, alone on the back patio one evening, I heard rustling noises in the bushes and what sounded like the unmistakeable grunting of pigs. The next moment, a herd of what looked like a gang of juvenile hoodlum hogs came barrelling through the foliage. They were of varying size, though none was much larger than a mid-sized dog. Some sported sharp tusks and gave off an offensive odour.

When I reported the incident to the owners of the place—who had heard the stories but never actually seen any of these animals—they were sceptical, but I did a little research and soon discovered that what I'd witnessed was not all that unusual in that part of the American Southwest. The marauders turned out to be pigs that had escaped from their enclosures years ago and now roamed the desert. They have even been given a name: the Arizona Javelina. Apparently, they are huge fans of the prickly pear cactus, which grows naturally beyond the fences of such gated communities but is even more abundant and succulent within their walls, where it is a popular landscaping item.

The way they develop these places is to strip the entire area of its natural vegetation, build the homes, and then sell the various indigenous plants, whether palm tree or cactus or shrub, back to the owners as part of a landscaping contract. When the wild pigs make their way into the compound, not only are they free to load up at a buffet of succulent cacti, but they have no predators to worry about while feasting. They're getting bolder, though, and it seems they may have moved on, not only from being nocturnal, but also from their strict diet of the prickly pear cactus, as they have been spotted of late walking down suburban neighbourhood streets in broad daylight nosing through the garbage containers.

CHAPTER FOUR

Scenes From a Barn

If as farmer fills his barn with grain, he gets mice.
If he leaves it empty, he gets actors.
WALTER SCOTT

A Place of Fear and Loathing

In the final scene of *The Grapes of Wrath* the Joad family has taken refuge inside a dilapidated barn, where they encounter a malnourished vagrant. Rose of Sharon has just lost her newborn baby and offers her breast milk to the starving man. It's a powerful scene that catches many readers with a lump in their throat, but for some reason leaves others put off. There seems to be a fundamental psychological divide between these two groups of people, but what exactly is it? Why does one reader find the scene "haunting" and "heartwarming" while the other characterizes it as "gross" or "cheap"? Freudian analysis might diagnose the latter with anal retentive issues, but is there an alternative interpretation? In her book, *Disgust: The Gatekeeper Emotion*, Susan Miller writes at length about the strong negative reaction this scene evokes in some people. She makes the case that people who are prone to react with disgust to certain situations or ideas are actually employing it as a coping mechanism. She sees it as a particularly effective weapon, often drawn like a gun, used by people with issues of narcissism. These are individuals who cannot, or will not, internalize or acknowledge their own capacity for weakness or fragility. Sound like someone you know? Anything that brings them too close to a realization of their own true nature must be projected onto others. The narcissist must love himself at all costs, for the alternative is self-loathing.

An Absolute Must-See

"Once you've seen the signs about the barn, it becomes impossible to see the barn." So says Murray Jay Siskind, a character in Don DeLillo's novel *White Noise.* He has taken a friend on a road trip to see "America's most photographed barn," which tourists come from everywhere to take pictures of. What is really going on, Murray explains, has less to do with any real barn than with conspicuous consumption. The many signs leading up to site of the so-called barn attest to this. Whatever the images that end up on the camera may be, they will take a back seat to the experience of having collected them.

You can witness this same phenomenon in places like the Grand Canyon, the Eiffel Tower, or walking the streets of a city like Venice: crowds of people posing with their smartphones, eager to post their presence at such a trendy spot to social media. Enter the room in the Louvre where the Mona Lisa hangs behind a thick pane of bulletproof glass and you quickly realize the painting itself is a secondary issue. Throngs of visitors jostle for position and mill about with one goal in mind: to take plenty of selfies. In a real sense they have not come to experience the painting. They are more interested in establishing the fact that they were in the same room with this iconic work of art. Why bother paying much attention to the Mona Lisa itself? Everyone already knows what it looks like.

The Ponte della Paglia is one of the many popular bridges that cross the canals of Venice. It's jammed with tourists during the day, most of them hustled off the gargantuan cruise ships that dock nearby. People crowd every square inch of the bridge, taking selfies of themselves standing on it. But here is the catch: many of them mistakenly think that they are standing on the Bridge of Sighs, a much more famous bridge situated nearby. It can be seen high above the canal, where it connects the Doge's Palace with a one-time prison. It gets its name from a story that tells of prisoners being taken from the palace to their cells after sentencing. They are allowed a final glimpse of beautiful Venice as they cross the bridge over the canal, and it causes them to let out a sigh.

"Standing on the Bridge of Sighs" reads the tagline on a photo posted to one social media site I visited. The image is of a woman who identifies herself as a celebrity fashion stylist posing on what is in fact the Ponte della Paglia. To make the faux pas even more tragic, she's leaning over the side of the bridge that faces the lagoon. If she'd chosen the other side at least the actual bridge might have made it into the background of the photo.

Get It Right and You Might Still Be Wrong

The most photographed barn in America might be the Moulton Barn, which can be found at the foot of the Rocky Mountains in Antelope Flats, Wyoming. It may not be a brilliant red, but it is ochre coloured and beautifully rustic-looking. The Grand Teton Mountain Range makes for an impressive backdrop, but if you google this barn, more than one version pops up in the images. One has a gable roof while the other is decidedly gambrel, and where the logs run vertically along the gable end of one, they run horizontally in another. It speaks pointedly to the idea in Don DeLillo's book. Perhaps even this "real" barn—as a single, distinct, entity—doesn't actually exist.

Pastiche, Anyone?

Barn scenes in movies—and there are a surprising number of them—almost always contain a stock inventory of standard features. Inside the dark interior there will be shafts of light coming in through the weathered boards, but it will be difficult to make things out, and there'll be plenty of nooks and corners where something might be lurking in the shadows. At some point a door will creak or possibly even slam shut. Other noises will be more difficult to interpret. Is that a cow groaning or slasher moaning?

The barn as depicted in slasher films often serves as a tried and true vessel for the fears we may secretly harbour. The irony is that we take comfort from them there, so long as we are scared along agreed-upon lines. Take "The Cat Scare" as it's known in the entertainment industry: lots of suspense builds up inside the unlit and cavernous barn until a sudden noise or leap startles the character who—contrary to even the most rudimentary principles of good judgement—has decided to investigate, but it quickly turns out to be nothing more than a flapping pigeon or a leaping cat. We knew it was coming, we anticipated it, and like the sudden steep drop on a roller coaster ride, it provided us with a delicious spark of excitement.

The barn scene is right up there as a cliché of immense utility. Like any good bromide it provides a buffer against the unsettling reality of everyday existence. It allows us to breathe. We don't have to think or interpret, just react. We've seen this movie before. And it is all quite harmless. Things are complicated out there these days and quite often unnerving, but a steady, reliable cliché is something you can count on. No surprises. It's the reason art in its highest form is often so difficult. We want to avoid having to do too much work. We don't want to be taken out of our comfort zone.

Freud in the Barn

The January 24, 1999 episode of *The Sopranos* opens with Tony Soprano sitting in the waiting room of his psychiatrist's office, staring intently at one of the paintings on the wall. The point of view switches and we look through Tony's eyes as he concentrates on the darkened doorway of the barn depicted there, the dim interior beyond its threshold. The longer he inspects the painting, the more unsettled he becomes, until, visibly upset, he confronts Doctor Melfi about it during their session. He accuses her of deliberately hanging the

A spooky barn AUTHOR WATERCOLOUR

picture of a "spooky, depressing barn" up there as a way of plumbing his psychological depths, employing it as a kind of Rorschach test, although he bungles the term and refers to it as a "Corshack" test.

Tony's paranoid insistence that he's being manipulated in this way by Dr. Melfi is laughable, but perhaps the notion that the doorway leading into the dim interior of a barn might serve as a pathway to the subconscious is not so far-fetched. Freudian analysis might employ the barn as a diagnostic tool to probe for certain traits and tendencies. One test might ask subjects whether they would prefer to spend time in a new barn, or an old one, and based on the choice they make, interpret certain pertinent aspects of their personality. Deeper investigation might examine the subject's preference for spending an hour in a barn either alone, or in the company of others.

Imagine you were given the option to actually live in a barn. Would you prefer an old one, or would it have to be spanking new?

What would your choice reveal about you? A word association test might distinguish between positive (organic, natural, wholesome) and negative (odorous, decaying, coarse) aspects. For my part, I find the prospect of setting up house in a new barn unappealing. Chances are it would lack a "soul," so I would opt for older one full of character. Does that make me pretentious or authentic?

Life, Imitates Art, Imitates …

Is there an act of violence that hasn't been committed in a barn? Whether it be something like *The Barn,* a throwback to eighties slasher movies, or Wes Craven's *Deadly Blessing,* the barn is often portrayed as a place of menace and outright evil. "What happens every year when the harvest moon shines its brightest?" You don't want to know. The murder weapon is often a pickaxe, but in the movie *Pitchfork,* a one-armed barn villain impales his victims with a prosthesis which takes the form of a pitchfork.

Murder In The Red Barn, a 1935 movie starring—I am not making this up—Todd Slaughter in the role of William Corder, is based on an actual murder case that occurred in Suffolk, England in 1827 that had all the elements of a crime of passion. You might wonder that they made a point of using the word red in the title, except that it is the same colour as blood, but apparently the barn was a local landmark known by that name. Corder shot and killed his lover, a young woman by the name of Maria Marten, inside the barn and then buried her body under the dirt floor. The barn became something of a tourist attraction and curious visitors stripped it bare of anything that might be considered a keepsake to commemorate the occasion. Speculation continues and people are still writing about what may have happened there that day. Songs and dramatic presentations depicting the event are still regularly performed in the region.

Then there were the Hinterkaifeck Murders in Bavaria. In that case an entire family of five, including the newly hired maid, were lured into the barn one by one and dispatched with a pickaxe.

When You Really Need One

I always thought what Uncle Jed and Granny and the rest of the gang from the Beverly Hillbillies really needed on that estate of theirs was a good old-fashioned barn. Think how much happier they would have been, especially Elly May with her love of animals continually on display. If Mr. Drysdale had used his influence to get one built for them, there would have been far fewer problems—and fewer episodes! I think Miss Hathaway would have loved it! To me, she came across as a farm girl at heart. Unfortunately, the closest thing to a barn was an episode where the gullible Clampetts mistook a bank raising for a barn raising.

If You Can Read This

Everything has a price, and some early farmers were not above taking advantage of the fact that the barn they had erected dominated the landscape. Before the advent of billboards, the side of a barn, especially if it could be seen from the highway, often became the site for commercial advertisements. The owner would be offered a free coat of paint in exchange for allowing the company to promote its product. Thus, the entire side of a barn, or perhaps the front gable, might serve to illustrate everything from a tin of snuff to a bottle of beer, a brick of butter to a sack of flour. Travellers driving by could be enticed to consider the merits of a particular brand of candy or can of ham, a flask of bourbon or a pouch of tobacco. Some of these advertisements can still be seen today, including a particularly fetching one I came across recently for a bottle of Coca-Cola on the side of a bright red barn. The two seemed like a perfect match. Other barns display the equivalent of a Velvet Elvis, with renditions of "The King" and other pop celebrities such as Marlon Brando, Johnny Cash, and The Beatles portrayed across them.

Occasionally the side of a barn can serve as canvas for a more serious work of art, such as the one in Wisconsin with a portrait of the Mona Lisa on it. You can find a recreation of Michelangelo's

The Creation on the side of an Iowa barn, and many more feature other iconic renaissance paintings. One Iowa barn features a clever parody of Grant Wood's *American Gothic*. The painting depicts a stern, almost menacing, farmer clutching a three-pronged pitchfork as he stares directly at the viewer. Standing next to him is his wife, grim of countenance, her gaze averted as she contemplates the sharp tines of the fork he holds before them. They stand out in the yard, the house prominent in behind them, but also visible in the picture on the right side is what looks like part of a faded red barn.

The painting has been parodied countless times in various other media, and while some viewers take issue with its severe depiction of rural folk, my criticism is that Mr. Wood might have done better to pose the couple in front of the barn. The man is holding a pitchfork after all, a symbol of the rural work ethic if there ever was one. He hasn't even bothered to put the damn thing down long enough to pose for the portrait, and it seems to me his wife is thinking as much while she stands dutifully, if sourly, next to him.

The pitchfork is of interest for several reasons. The structure of the entire painting is composed around it. Its tripartite design can be seen reflected in the window behind them, and again in the shirt the farmer is wearing. There's more than a hint of suggestion it might be put to more menacing use than merely throwing around some hay. It certainly wouldn't be the first time. In many a movie it is often the weapon of choice for mobs of angry peasants, along with the scythe and the axe, as they storm the castle walls. Indeed, there is an entire protocol for their display in some barns, where they are hung along the wall in rows, like so many rifles in an armory.

CHAPTER FIVE

Pop Goes the Barn

There is a way children enter garages, barns, attics, the
same way they enter great halls, and family chapels.
LEONARD COHEN

And on That Farm There Was a …

The who's who of the barnyard can be summed up in that old children's classic, "Old Macdonald Had a Farm." The shortlist almost always includes a cow, a horse, a lamb, a chick, a pig, a duck, and maybe a dog or a cat. The list of popular singers who've taken it upon themselves (although I like to think it had more to do with the terms of the contract they were working under) to offer various renditions of this song is really quite astonishing. Frank Sinatra kicked out a version that had a "chick" strutting around the barnyard distracting all the horny young farmhands from their work. It was done in a jazzy style, a variation that conjures up Bobby Darin singing "Mack The Knife," complete with a key change after every chorus.

Elvis Presley sang a version of the song in the movie *Double Trouble* while sitting next to an attentive young woman on the back of a farm truck loaded with crated chickens. The lyrics had once again been modified of course, and somehow managed to be both playful and bloody-minded at the same time. The verse about the pigs starts out as follows:

Old Macdonald had a farm
ee-i-ee-i-o
And on that farm, he had some pigs
ee-i-ee-i-o
With an oink, oink, here, an oink, oink there
Pigs everywhere in sight …

And here the lyrics suddenly change to warn the pigs that if they don't behave right, there'll be pork and beans that night! A similar fate awaits other barnyard animals who might dare to be disobedient. If the cows get "out of line" they become hamburger, while the hens become chicken fricassee. The story goes that Elvis was so incensed at having to perform this ridiculous musical number that he had a major meltdown with the movie studio. Other people who have done a version of this song include Ella Fitzgerald, Flatt and Scruggs, and Alvin and the Chipmunks.

Suuuuiieeeeeee

There's a long tradition of fictionalizing barnyard animals in movies, books, and cartoons. Give the cows and horses, sheep and chickens their due, but in the end they all take a back seat to the pig. Look no further than literature and film to see how often it is this creature that plays a prominent role. Think of Wilbur in E.B. White's *Charlotte's Web,* Piglet from *Winnie The Pooh* fame, or Miss Piggy of *The Muppets.* George Orwell chose an assortment of swine to lead the revolt on drunken farmer Jones in *Animal Farm.* Babe, star of the movie by the same name, became so popular they had to put out a sequel. Then there's Arnold from *Green Acres,* the three little pigs, and of course Porky Pig. Throw in Hamm, the talking piggy bank in *Toy Story,* and the case for the pig is all but ironclad.

In the recent children's movie *Barnyard,* the opening shot pans down from the title to a stereotypical farm scene with one noteworthy exception, namely the animators' decision to literally put teats on a bull. The studio execs were somehow convinced that children tended to think of bulls as a different species from cows, a distinction they considered a problem. The solution was to render the bulls as male "cows" and replace their genitalia with an udder, situated more or less where the male naughty bits would normally be displayed. Watching the scene where a bunch of them stand around on two legs, elbows propped on the railing of the fence as they engage in typical "guy" talk, is unsettling. The sight of their udders hanging down in front tests the cartoon limits of suspension of disbelief.

In one scene the main character, Otis (voiced over by comic actor Kevin James), prepares to perform an acrobatic stunt, but first requests that he be allowed to take a "hit" from the salt lick. The musical score makes ample use of the banjo and the characters in the movie have also been marketed as a video game. In another scene the farm animals (mainly cows and pigs) prop up the farmer (who has been rendered unconscious) under a tree and put a book in his hand to make it look as if he's fallen asleep while reading. The book? *Charlotte's Web*.

Typecasting Tropes

Perhaps the reason for the popularity of barnyard animals as fictional (and sometimes even literary) characters has to do with the nagging suspicion that they are more sentient than we want to believe. It may be more comfortable to anthropomorphize them in a simplistic way, and the stereotypes that have developed over the years serve just that purpose. Horses inevitably tend to be hard-working and steady of character. Cows are amiable but not terribly bright, and sheep are easily led. Chickens tend to be skittish and gossipy. Then there are the pets, such as the aloof cat and the loyal dog. Let's not forget the stubborn donkey and the greedy pig. And what about the peripherals—animals indirectly connected to the barnyard—such as the bloodthirsty bat, the wily fox, the dirty rat, the sneaky weasel, and the thieving magpie? Throw in the wise (old) owl and the skittish pigeon and the list is all but complete.

There's a recent trend to deliberately go against these familiar (and tired) barnyard tropes, and especially popular is the demonic domestic. Almost any barnyard animal can be demonized—just add fangs, sunken red eyes, and deep wrinkles. Marvel Comics has developed a character named Bessie, better known as Hellcow, who produces vampire milk. The backstory is that she was preyed upon by Count Dracula when she lived on a Swiss farm and now she travels the globe seeking revenge. She wears a cape and has super-bovine strength and agility.

In a Pig's Sty

There's a fair bit of wallowing with the pigs in the movies. When Clint Eastwood falls face-first in some sloppy hog manure at his ramshackle farm, it acts as the catalyst that turns him back into a gunfighter in *Unforgiven*. In *The Wizard of Oz*, Dorothy falls into a pigsty attached to the barn but is soon rescued by one of the farm hands, without even a spot of manure on her backside. In *Scarecrow*, a bit of a reverse riff on Steinbeck's *Of Mice and Men* (instead of a little farm for George and Lennie it's a carwash for Max and Francis), Gene Hackman agrees to work in the pigsty for the chance to beat up the man who brutalized his travelling companion, Al Pacino. In the Italian film *Pigsty,* one of the characters prefers the company of pigs to humans but ends up being eaten by them. This also happens in *Hannibal*, and another movie titled *PigPen*.

Bond in the Barn

There are certain prerequisites a set decorator is sure to include for a barn scene in any movie. When James Bond (Sean Connery) finds himself in that setting accompanied by Pussy Galore (Honor Blackman) in *Goldfinger,* the requisite hay manger plays a prominent role, as might be expected. In *On Her Majesty's Service,* Bond (George Lazenby this time) gets cozy with Tracy di Vicenzo (Diana Rigg) in much the same manner, but this time James takes the unorthodox step of proposing to his Bond girl and so proper decorum is observed, at least for a little while. The two set off to sleep in separate mangers but it doesn't last more than a few seconds before, well, Bond does what Bond does.

Before they were Bond girls both actors starred in the television series *The Avengers* with Patrick Macnee (Honor Blackman was Cathy Gale and Dianna Rigg was Emma Peel). That show took a distinctly feminist approach to the roles of its female stars. Many people wondered why Patrick Macnee never got cast as James Bond. He was a friend of Ian Fleming's but apparently didn't care for the character of Bond as portrayed in his books. He did play a role in *A View to a Kill* and narrated a number of Bond special feature videos.

Ironically, Sean Connery played the villain in the movie version of *The Avengers*, while the role of John Steed was played by Ralph Fiennes, who of course plays "M" in the most recent Bond films. One of the cars John Steed drove in *The (New) Avengers*, a 1976 Jaguar XJ12 C, turned up years later and was considered a "barn find." It sold at auction for just under $100,000.

Inadvertent Sculpture

When it comes to barnyard animals, it is the commercial salt lick—a slab or brick about the size of a car battery—that serves as their source of sodium chloride, and cows in particular seem to enjoy using their abrasive tongues to take in their daily dose. They have a particular need for it because it is important to the production of milk, which contains sodium as well as chloride. They have an instinctive craving for it, and when they don't get enough, they resort to some pretty weird behaviors. They will chew on wood, lick at carcasses, drink mud, chomp on animal bones, and even lick up their urine just to get their daily dose.

As the animals lick the block of salt with their coarse tongues, they sometimes form interesting hollows and swirling curves into the block. Observant farmers have made note of salt licks in their barns and pastures that resemble modern-day abstract sculpture, and in

Baker City, Oregon they hold a popular annual contest known as The Great Salt Lick, in which salt blocks that have been licked into various pleasing aesthetic forms are put on display. There's a running competition among annual contestants as to which make the better finished product—sheep or cows. In other places salt licks are put out expressly for the purpose of making art.

Sorry about Your Barn

In *Back to the Future*, when young Marty McFly arrives in his time-travelling DeLorean, he makes his entrance by crashing into Farmer Peabody's barn. We watch him disembark from the straw-covered DeLorean to the accompaniment of mooing cows and squawking chickens. The commotion brings the gormless farmer and his family out to investigate and when they see young Marty in his hazmat suit, they take him for an alien stepping out of a flying saucer and flee the scene. By the time Marty emerges through the door of the dusty barn, Farmer Peabody has made a quick trip back to the house for his shotgun. Marty, being the polite and properly raised Midwestern young lad that he is, apologizes for any damage he may have inadvertently caused, at which Farmer Peabody lets loose with his twelve gauge. In the course of making his getaway, Marty takes out a newly planted tree with his time-travelling car and the farmer yells after him, "You space bastard! You killed my pine!" It's an unflattering treatment of rural folk, but typical of the tropes common to barns and their owners in movies.

If Not for the Barn

Barns play an important role in a surprising number of scenes when it comes to film, but it's also true for books and comics. Clark Kent would never have become Superman if he hadn't gone out to the barn one night and lifted the straw-covered trap door to unearth the eerily glowing green spire his father Jor-El had sent along with him to Earth. In *Of Mice and Men*, if poor Curley's wife (Steinbeck didn't bother giving her a name) hadn't wandered into the barn and got Lennie all riled up with her feminine wanton ways she might have made it safely to Hollywood. The 1939 movie version of *Of Mice and Men* (barn scene) was up against *The Wizard of Oz* (barn scene) for best picture at the Oscars that year. Also in the running was *Gone with the Wind*, which won. There was the no barn scene in that movie, but Sidney Howard, who wrote the screenplay, was killed in a farming accident when the tractor he was trying to crank-start lurched forward and pinned him against the wall of his barn. Also, the sets for the movie were discovered hidden away for the better part of thirty years inside a barn in the southern countryside not far from Atlanta, Georgia near Margaret Mitchell's ancestral home, the original setting for Tara in the novel.

From Tending the Rabbits to the Emerald City

There are some interesting parallels in the storylines of *The Wizard of Oz* and *Of Mice and Men*. Both Lennie and Dorothy long for a place where they won't get into any trouble. Dorothy leans against a haystack next to the barn and sings dreamily of a place at the end of the rainbow where "troubles melt like lemon drops." George and Lennie dream of a little farm with some cows and chickens where they can "live off the fat of the land." All Lennie wants to do is tend the rabbits.

When Dorothy embarks on a quest to reach the Emerald City, at first there's only herself and the Scarecrow, but pretty soon the Tin Man and then the Cowardly Lion ask to join. In *Of Mice and Men* it's just George and Lennie at first, until Candy asks if he can get in on the plan, and then Crooks wants a chance to join them as well. In both stories all of the characters are deficient in one aspect or another, from the Cowardly Lion's lack of courage to Crook's lack of a healthy spine. Just as the plans for the little farm never come to fruition, the Emerald City turns out to be a disappointment. "Guys like us," George explains to Lennie, "don't belong no place." But for Dorothy, "There's no place like home."

This barn features many traditional elements, including a gambrel roof, cross-hatched double doors, and a cupola. AUTHOR SKETCH

Yes, But is it Barnworthy?

Other movies with barn scenes include *High Plains Drifter* with Clint Eastwood, *Witness* with Harrison Ford, and Thomas Hardy's *Far from the Madding Crowd*. The short story "Barn Burning" by William Faulkner starts with a hog that keeps escaping the barnyard. There are songs called "Out Behind the Barn" by Little Jimmy Dickens, "Murder in the Red Barn" by Tom Waits, and "Hell in the Henhouse, Blood in the Barn" by Ray Wylie Hubbard. More than one early movie musical featured an old barn that was spruced up to become the venue for an amateur theatrical song and dance production. The show would be sure to draw a big audience and the money it brought in would be enough to save the orphanage.

Barn Movies

There's a silly game you can play in which you substitute the word "barn" for one of the words in the title of a movie or song or book.

Here are a few examples to get you started: *My Big Fat Barn Wedding, It's a Wonderful Barn, From Here to the Barn, Rebel Without a Barn, No Country for Old Barns, One Upon a Time in the Barn, The Silence of the Barns, Eternal Sunshine of the Spotless Barn, About a Barn …* you get the idea.

CHAPTER SIX

Back in the Day

*There are not many of these old barns left ...they belong
not to the living, busy, present, but to a different order of
things that can never come back to us from the past.*

GERTRUDE LEFFERTS VANDERBILT

Worth Its Weight in Gold

A dovecote is a barn designed to house pigeons. It has a long history
that goes all the back to ancient Roman times. In medieval Europe,
pigeons were bred and kept not only as a source of meat and eggs, but
also as a valued source of dung. It wasn't unusual for a dovecote to
have an armed guard stationed next to it in order to prevent anyone
from trying to steal the precious droppings inside, which was much
prized as a fertilizer and said to be spectacularly effective on melons
and cucumbers. The droppings were also a source of saltpetre, an
ingredient necessary for the manufacture of gunpowder.

During the nineteen-twenties dovecotes were a popular accessory
on the homes wealthy people built in the suburbs of cities like Los
Angeles and San Francisco. These storybook houses often resembled
something out of a fairy tale like *Snow White* or *Hansel and Gretel*
with whimsical, cottage-like architecture and odd-shaped, ridiculously
steep and pointy rooflines.

The dovecote in my father's house AUTHOR PHOTO

We discovered a dovecote in the turret of the derelict Victorian house my father lived in during his declining years. He bought the house shortly after he decided to give up farming to move into the city. He had lost most of his fortune by then, and most of his family. There were a lot of rooms in that old place, which had long ago been converted into a boarding house. By the time my father came along, it was so run down that only a few alcoholic boarders remained. They, too, would be gone soon and my father would spend the rest of his life—not counting some time in hospital and a couple of shabby care homes—living in self-imposed solitude inside his crumbling fortress. The house was located in a very bad part of town, surrounded by crack houses and gang hangouts and brothels, and after the last of the renters left, he stopped paying the bills. His heat and electricity were cut off, but he managed to somehow survive the Canadian Prairie winters by blocking himself off in only a couple of rooms and keeping them warm enough not to freeze. One of us would go over there every week or so to see if he was all right. When it was my turn, I'd go and bang on the big steel door he'd installed and there was never an answer. I would walk around the outside of the house to try and see into the dim interior for any sign of life. I'd leave a note on the door for him to call and then go home to my family. Was there ever a more warm and welcoming sight in all the world than my own front door after a trip like that?

Then one day we received a call that he was in the hospital, very weak and unable to walk. We found out that he had been crawling around inside the house on his knees for weeks until he finally dragged himself outside to summon help. He stayed in the hospital for some time and then went into a care home, but his strength never returned. When it became clear he was near the end, we all went to see him. My sisters, who were schoolteachers, promptly prepared a schedule for us to take turns staying with him. I drew the first shift. The others had only just left when he took a turn for the worse. I thought of trying to catch them before they left, but I could see he was slipping away. I did the only thing I could think of and took up his bony and withered hand in mine. I had never experienced the touch of my father's hand, not even as a child. I said something but it wasn't anything heart-wrenching or heartwarming. Nothing about forgiveness or atonement. Nothing you could use in a book or movie script. No revelations or epiphanies. What was there to say? Perhaps a barn cliché might have been appropriate: "The horse had left the barn a long time ago." Or maybe: "Why close the barn door after the horse has gone."

After the funeral we went to the house. Nobody had been allowed inside for some time. We knew it was going to be bad, but the conditions inside the house were almost beyond comprehension. A nightmare of hoarding and squalor. One of my sisters took a series of photographs but I don't like to look at them. It's too much. Rooms filled floor to ceiling with junk. One day we discovered a room quite by accident. We had no idea it was there until we uncovered the door behind a mountain of debris and clutter. It would have been nice to discover something of real value in there, but it was just more worthless rubbish.

When at last I fought my way through the detritus up to the third floor, I was startled by a flock of pigeons that flew up in a great noise and out through the broken windows of the turret. The floor was hidden under a deep layer of bird droppings, smooth and slippery. I knew my father couldn't have made it up there for some time. The pigeons, having gained access to the neglected upper floors of the great house through the broken windows, had turned the turret into a dovecote. The quantity of pigeon droppings was quite unbelievable. The smell was sour, damp, and vaguely swamp-like. It was an odour of ruin, neglect, decay, and failure. In ancient times it would have amounted to a motherlode. Just think: if my father he had been alive in medieval times he might have been able to generate enough income from all those droppings to get his electricity hooked up again.

Git Along, Little Gobbler

Cattle drives are the subject of many a movie from *City Slickers* to *Red River*, but it could just as well be chickens and turkeys instead of cows. In the nineteenth century, great poultry drives were commonplace and thousands of birds would be brought to market that way. Just as with cattle, they would stop for the night and the birds would sometimes roost in nearby barns in such numbers that the beams and rafters would collapse under their collective weight. The methodology was also somewhat different. Rather than a bunch of cowpokes on horseback whistling and waving their dusty hats, the drovers would employ kids to scatter feed in front of the birds and lure them in the direction they needed to go. Covered bridges could be a problem because their instinct not to travel at night would cause the turkeys making their way across to mistake the dim interior for dusk and simply stop. The only solution would be to pick them up individually and carry them out into the light where they would start up again. Needless to say, a journey of no more than a hundred miles could take many days.

A Barn by Any Other Name

Many of us are not all that far removed from living in a barn—or a housebarn at any rate. If you don't think there's a housebarn in your past, think again. They date back to prehistoric times, and this may be the reason why some people feel such a deep connection. Perhaps something in the collective unconscious links us to these places. You can still find these types of buildings carefully preserved in many European countries, and each language has a name for them. In Austria it's the *Zwerchhof*, Belgians had the *Langgevelboerderijen*. The Swiss lived in a *Engadinerhaus* or *chalet*, Estonians in a *Rehielamu*, Germans in a *Wohnstallhaus*, Spanish people in a *Baserri*, and the Dutch in a *los hoes boerderij*.

The reasons my Mennonite (Dutch) forebears opted for the housebarn were not much different, I imagine, from those of other European inhabitants. There was heat from the animals, safety from thieves and predators, easier monitoring of animals giving birth or undergoing medical issues. Of course, there was the problem of pests and vermin, and this is where the domestication of cats and dogs became handy. Dogs in particular were useful for catching rats, protecting the livestock, and acting as an alarm against intruders. Cats got away with more of a recreational existence in the barnyard, and even today they serve as more of an ornamental feature there. They may poach the odd mouse or swallow, but there are no breeds of "working cats." The record for a rat terrier, by the way, is something like twenty-five hundred rats in a span of seven hours. That's over three hundred rats an hour—or about five rats a minute. Kind of gives a whole other meaning to the notion of earning your keep.

Dogs had a lot of different jobs on the farm at one time. "Turnspit" dogs were placed on a small treadmill and made to operate various pieces of machinery. Others were used as draft animals and employed

A fine example of a traditional housebarn, one of a number still to be found in Mennonite villages of southern Manitoba AUTHOR PHOTO

to pull small carts or sleds. They still work today at herding animals like sheep and cattle, and to a lesser extent are trained to do the same with chickens and other poultry. On some farms they use border collies to herd turkeys, but things can easily go wrong. The birds can be notoriously difficult to move en masse from one location to another. If just one of them decides to cut and run back the way it came, the entire flock will stubbornly follow and then you have a full-blown turkey stampede on your hands.

There's something inherently funny sounding about this idea and I had a brother-in-law who positively guffawed the first time I mentioned it. I admit the two words do seem incongruous. Cattle stampede? Okay. Buffalo stampede? Sure. I'll even throw in wildebeests if you like. But a turkey stampede? Under the right circumstances, yes.

My father's infamous barn was spacious enough to hold the entire population of turkeys in inclement weather, and also when they had been spooked by some airborne menace and retreated into the barn for safety. Entry was accommodated by a row of intermittent hinged apertures that ran along either side of the barn through which they could scuttle in and out when inclined to do so. But if they were roving about out on the range and something really panicked them, things could quickly escalate. The result was a full-blown turkey stampede so intense that they would crowd against the relatively small openings in the side of the barn and begin to pile up, one on top of the other, in such numbers that many unfortunate birds at the bottom were asphyxiated.

Back at the original site of the barn, my father had at one point sought an injunction against an American who made a habit of repeatedly flying his small private aircraft over the turkeys (to the delight of the neighbouring farmers, no doubt), invariably putting them into a panic that resulted in the loss of many birds. It was the kind of thing that would eventually turn my father into a full-blown conspiracy theorist. Having been allowed through selective breeding to become extremely dimwitted, not to mention poor of eyesight, the turkeys mistook—again and again—any low-flying aircraft for a raptor of some kind. They couldn't tell a hawk from a handsaw, as Shakespeare might have put it, and certainly not from a Piper Cub airplane, so that the trick worked again and again.

Tarzan of the Turkeys

Imagine my delight when I discovered quite by accident one brilliant summer morning that I could affect very much the same result as the airplane simply by emitting a loud and high-pitched trill from my throat. I have no recollection of deliberately trying to come up with this ability, but the first time it happened the feeling of power it gave me was exhilarating. Suddenly, I could make an entire flock of ten thousand turkeys run for the barn with the simple force of my vocal cords. The best way I can describe the sound is by referring to one of my favourite movies of all time: *Lawrence of Arabia*. There's a scene where the Arab men are riding off into battle on their horses and camels while veiled women line the cliffs on either side and ululate, emitting a series of long, wavering, high-pitched sounds as a send-off to their men. The sound I could make, and still can, is harsher, louder, and more forceful, and must be sustained for a fairly long period of time at high pitch, volume, and intensity to have the desired effect. There is something of a delayed reaction. It's as if the birds begin to communicate with each other when they hear it and spend some time trying to figure out exactly what they ought to do about it.

The unspoken turkey conversation might have gone something like this:

"Are you hearing this?"

"You bet I am."

"What the hell is it?'

"I don't know but it's freaking me out."

"Where is it coming from?"

"Hard to say. Up there, maybe?"

By now the birds would all be standing stock still with their neck craned, heads cocked to one side staring up into the sky.

"You see anything up there?'

"Nope. Do you?"

"Nope."

"Well I am getting seriously spooked."

"Me, too."

"Wanna make a run for it?"

"I think it might be best."

"Last one in the barn is a rotten egg." (Where does this expression originate?)

Once a few birds decided to bolt for the barn the race was on, and pretty soon ten thousand birds would be on the run.

I think the first thing that strikes me now about this phenomenon is how I stumbled upon it. I have searched the internet and found not a shred of evidence that it has ever been replicated. There are videos of people in turkey enclosures with thousands of birds doing some pretty funny things and getting some interesting responses. But there's nothing like the sound I could generate, and as far as I know I am still the only human capable of making it. I don't think it wise to reveal too much about how to produce it. If I go into too much detail, someone reading this might learn how to make the noise and try it out on a flock of turkeys, which might set off a stampede with tragic results. I'm only half kidding.

Somebody's Gotta Do It

There have always been plenty of chores barn do around the barnyard: milking, feeding, shovelling, pitching, hauling, carrying, sweeping, washing, tending, filling, emptying, harnessing, mending. In the popular television series *Dirty Jobs,* Mike Rowe shot a number of episodes on the farm. He carried out such farm chores as sexing chickens, collecting alligator eggs, processing onions, shearing alpacas, castrating sheep, plucking feathers, and cleaning hooves. The various types of farms he worked on included an ostrich farm, a pig farm, a worm dung farm, a mushroom farm, an alligator farm, a maggot farm, a cricket farm, and a reindeer farm.

For a time, my older brother ran a farm I worked on. He kept a few pigs, big ones, that would breed and produce offspring, and once in a while one could be slaughtered for meat. They were poorly housed and got out all the time, at which point they would go rooting about the yard, tearing up the grass and what passed for a lawn, not to mention digging up my sister-in-law's garden. Pigs of any size have a powerful, sturdy, shovel-shaped snout and even a few of them can do an unbelievable amount of damage in a short while as they go about rooting out whatever interests them.

I would run around chasing after them to get them back into the pen. There was only one way to do this. You couldn't tackle a four-hundred-pound pig and drag it back to the barn. They were too strong and too agile. But you could tire them out. Pigs, it turns out, do not have a particularly robust cardiovascular system. It tends to deteriorate rapidly, and because I was in good physical condition, I simply outlasted them. I would run one down, grab on and let it drag me around for a bit to tire it out even more, then simply grab it by the ear and lead it back to the barn. The pigs were surprisingly compliant once they had been brought to a state of exhaustion and by this means I managed to get them all back into their enclosure.

That part of the chores was relatively enjoyable and even satisfying to a degree, but feeding time was something altogether different. The hogs were separated into a number of pens for various reasons that had to do with breeding, infighting, disease, etc. I would come by with a couple of pails full of shredded oats and as soon as they saw me, they would break into the most piercing squeals and grunts to see if it might get them fed first. The more zealous ones would lift themselves up onto the top rail of the pen so that their hooves hung over the edge and squeal for all they were worth. The decibel level, I'm certain, exceeded safety standards.

Old Macdonald's Ten Axioms of the Barnyard

1. In order for the barn to become clean the farmer must become dirty.

2. The ratio of chores already done to chores still pending remains constant.

3. In the event that the cow's tail knocks your cap off, it will land in the gutter.

4. The cow will drop a steaming load only *after* it has entered the barn.

5. You will spot the runaway pig just as it roots out the last garden potato.

6. No barn door has ever come off its railings in good weather.

7. The tractor will break down in the field farthest from the farmyard.

8. Daylight remaining will always be a little less than the time needed to finish the job.

9. The manure left to shovel up will be a bit more than the last wheelbarrow can hold.

10. The cow will manage to kick over the bucket just as you finish the milking.

Fork It Over

The barn is a place of hand tools and implements, so much so that many barns feature a tool shed or a workshop dedicated especially to that purpose. Here, repairs can be made to machinery that has broken down, or to some part of the infrastructure that needs mending. Such a shop will often have a sturdy workbench cluttered with tools of every use and description. A quick inspection reveals chisels, files, rasps, planers, saws, hand drills, punches, screwdrivers, pliers, mallets, at least one gooseneck, and a claw hammer or two. Among items hung on the wall or leaned into the far corner of the shop will be axe and sledgehammer, crowbar and pickaxe, rake and spade. Out in the barn itself, either hung on racks or leaned here and there at various strategic locations, will be bale hooks, shovels, pails and stools, and most important of all, a range of pitchforks. Of all the tools it takes to make the barnyard function properly, the pitchfork wins hands down. You simply can't have a barn without a variety of them. There are a number of variations to this quintessential implement, each one designed for a particular purpose—lots of tines, for example, if you're going to be handling manure, and only a few if you're pitching hay up into the loft.

So Much Depends ...

Another indispensable barnyard implement is the wheelbarrow, which originated in China about two thousand years ago. It may originally have been designed for use in wartime to supply troops and was

This old Tuscan wheelbarrow has made thousands of trips across olive groves, farm fields, and barnyards, carrying everything from apples to firewood to manure. AUTHOR PHOTO

especially handy in wet and muddy conditions. In case of attack, a fleet of them could be arranged in a circle for defense purposes. The famous call to "Get all the wagons in a circle!" associated with American westerns might have originated in China as a command to round up all the wheelbarrows. There's evidence that some wheelbarrows might even have had weaponry installed on them, much as future military campaigns would feature pieces of artillery mounted on two wheels. They also had a particularly interesting innovation on some of their barrows, which consisted of a sail mounted on a mast at the front end of the barrow for wind-assisted transportation.

Wheelbarrows made their appearance in Europe sometime around the beginning of the thirteenth century after visitors to the Far East brought the idea back with them. The first written reference to a wheelbarrow dates to an order of purchase in 1222. These days you can go out and buy a power-assisted wheelbarrow that operates on electricity, an idea that originated in Japan. It's a bit like a variation on a Segway because it's a "smart" machine that senses how much assistance is needed, depending on the weight of the load and the force being exerted by the operator.

The wheelbarrow may be to the barnyard what the bicycle is to the city. There's something aesthetically pleasing about them. Lots of artists like to put them in their paintings, but I somehow managed to miss the one of a woman rolling a wheelbarrow down a medieval roadway on my visit to the Louvre, not to mention the nineteenth-century portrait of a grossly obese Englishman totting his stomach before him in a wheelbarrow at the British Museum. There's no telling what you can miss when you're not looking for it. There's even poetry about the wheelbarrow, and one of the finest was penned by William Carlos Williams.

You can get a tremendous amount of work done with a good wheelbarrow. Its unique design makes it appear crude and primitive, but it's amazingly efficient. I can attest to spending an inordinate amount time and effort hauling various commodities from one place to another in a wheelbarrow: dirt, gravel, animal carcasses, manure, motors, transmissions, all manner of machinery, scrap metal, siblings, piglets, chicks, water, snow, ice, hay, straw, clothing, electronics, wood, ashes, tires, leaves, barbed wire, fence posts, tools, newspapers, shingles, bottles, cans, grandfathers and friends. But never my own stomach.

A Home Away from Home

In Spain you can find buildings called *parideras* which were not part of the farmyard but located in remote areas of the open countryside. Some were formed from natural caves, but usually they were constructed from stone and rough wooden timbers and finished off with a terracotta roof. Many of the ones still in good condition have been converted into houses or hotels, but their original function was to offer protection from predators for herds of sheep or cows or goats, and to serve as places of shelter in bad weather. They could also be a safe place for an animal to give birth, and the manure which accumulated inside was sometimes sold or used as fertilizer.

CHAPTER SEVEN

The Repurposed Barn

*I compare myself to a good barn. You can have a good
barn, and if you paint it, it looks a little better. But
if you take the paint off, it's still a good barn.*
DOLLY PARTON

Here Come the City Slickers

It seems the barn aesthetic is something of a fad these days. Trendy urbanites like to drive out into the country, strip the weathered boards off old barns and use them to decorate their high-rise condos. Others simply order the salvaged material online and have it installed in their lofts. Barn doors that hang from an overhead rail and slide open with an easy push are a particularly popular item. Accessories to round out the look include bar stools made out of old tractor seats and pitchfork tines repurposed as pot hangers. How about a set of chairs with the seats and backs made out of old shovel blades, or kitchen stools fashioned out of large gears salvaged from discarded pieces of old farm machinery? Stick a rounded piece of tempered glass on an old wagon wheel, add the legs, and you have a chic coffee table. Pound rusty old nails into the front of your outdoor siding to display your house number. Turn old barn siding into shelving for books. Line up a bunch of shovel handles to make a back for your rustic couch. Weld

The gable end of this repurposed barn retains some of the original features, although the opening to the loft has been converted into a set of French doors.
COURTESY HAROLD NEUFELD

old wrenches into a square for a picture frame. Turn a milk can into a flowerpot. Nail a rake to the wall and hang wine glasses by their stems between the tines. Use heavy iron braces for bookends. Make campy shelving out of grain auger blades. And on and on ...

Wagon Wheel Surprise

If you drive away from the city and look out through the window of your car at an old farm wagon piled high with straw you think—ahh, how quaint and nostalgic it all is. If you happen to live on that farm and you look out the window you think, "There's a lot of work there."

These days vintage farm wagons once used for hauling hay into the barn sell for a good deal of money. You can get one with a

Columbus Box, or a one-horse swab wagon, a freight wagon, even a chuck wagon. The wagon wheels are a big item, too. People make chandeliers out of them, put them out in the yard and plant flowers in between the spokes, fashion wine racks, cut the wheel in half and use the two sides for the legs on a coffee table, mount one over the stove in the kitchen to hang pots from, construct a giant wall clock, make a glass-topped kitchen table, or use one as a gate for the fence. Or you can just lean it against the wall.

Actually, I Was Raised in a Barn

You can set up house in a barn if you choose. There are apartments for rent conveniently situated above working barns, where tenants can go down the stairs to work with horses and other animals. The idea is hardly a new one, and in some southern European regions people have been living above their barns for centuries. Many are constructed out of thick slabs of stone around a walled-in enclosure, with the living quarters above the animal pens. These days it's become fashionable for many owners to gut and renovate the barn portion and convert it into an apartment for sale or rent. They often come with an added swimming pool because of the hot summers. On Gozo, an island off the coast of Malta in the Mediterranean, there are so many of them that a number of websites have sprung up dedicated exclusively to marketing these converted barns. There's a wealth of places to choose from, but bring your wallet as the place is going to run you upwards of three hundred Euros per night.

One of the big companies in barn design in North America is Barn Pros. They offer to design and build you a functioning barn with a loft that can serve as your home. If you want to start from scratch, you can order re-engineered barn home kits ready to be assembled. Go to any state or province, any European country, and you will find people living in barns. Sometimes they have been built from scratch, other times old barns have been restored to serve as comfortable living spaces with tremendous character. They combine rustic flavour with touches of the luxurious. Some of them are stunningly beautiful restorations and conversions of classic red barns. Others are opulent and some even glamorous, referred to as barndominiums, which can be lived in or rented out.

Occasionally the makeover doesn't go so well. A recent headline in the *Telegraph* reads: "Bad Barn Conversions a Rural Cancer." The subtitle mentions "A visual rape of the country-side that cannot be undone." Apparently there is a lot of "inappropriate" renovation going on, whether it be to wagon sheds, byres (for keeping cows), dovecotes (for the housing of pigeons—often built out of stone and resembling nothing so much as a place where a family of elves might dwell), stables, or oat houses (barn-like buildings constructed for the purpose of drying and storing hops). There are complaints about "horror" barn conversions that contribute to the "suburbanization of the country-side."

Some people take their barns very seriously, and the internet is full of sites where an individual or organization is trying to enlist the services of crowdfunding platforms to save one barn or another. Some of these organizations are quite advanced. The National Barn Alliance seeks to "provide national leadership for the preservation of America's historic barns and rural heritage through education, documentation, conservation, and networking." They have a newsletter, *The Barn Door*, that you can subscribe to. There are films, books, classroom programs, and of course plenty of presence on social media including an official blog, *The Barn Journal*.

I've mentioned that I'm from a Mennonite background and that my ancestors lived for centuries in dwellings where the house and barn were attached. A few of these buildings still stand where they were first built, in the villages that dot the Red River Valley of southern Manitoba. Some have fallen into disrepair and neglect, while others have benefitted from regular maintenance and repair. The village of Neubergthal boasts a number of housebarns that have been meticulously preserved or restored, in fact the entire village has been declared a National Historic Site. Visitors there can enjoy an idyllic

The Krahn Barn. The family resides on the main floor, while the spacious loft above serves as a venue for a variety of events. COURTESY MARGRUITE KRAHN

setting of picturesque housebarns neatly arranged along either side of a single tree-lined street.

The beams on these old barns were hewn out of solid oak timbers well over a hundred years ago, and the wood has become so solid it's all but impossible to drive a nail into one without bending it in half. One couple I know there have spent a great deal of time and energy fixing up a barn that now serves quite nicely as a home for the entire family, while the loft overhead can be used as a venue for musical acts, author readings, and other events. I like the way they went our predecessors one better, and instead of living in a house attached to a barn, they live *in* the barn. It's known as the Krahn Barn, owned by Margruite and Paul Krahn, and you can visit them on Facebook.

Writers in particular seem to have affection for the barn as a working and living space. Cormac McCarthy bought a barn near

Louisville, Tennessee not far from Knoxville, and renovated the entire building before moving in and writing some of his finest work within its walls. The author Verlyn Klinkenborg, who has written some very fine pieces on barns and rural life in general for *The New York Times*, regularly holds writing workshops in a barn. Then there's Lane Smith, the children's writer. Ernest Hemingway had a writing studio that was a converted barn. It's a museum now, in Piggott, Arkansas. Hemingway did quite a lot of writing there, thanks to the generosity of the wealthy Pfeiffer family, which he married into after he met Pauline Pfeiffer at a party in Paris. Apparently, Hemingway had a habit of squandering the money he made from his latest book on extravagant living and when it ran out, he would make his way back to Piggott and wheedle some money out of his relatives. In fact, it was the Pfeiffer family that financed his African safari. The locals considered him something of a freeloader and weren't sorry to see him go.

Barn as Therapy

There's been a recent explosion in the development of programs where individuals with varying disorders (they range from psychiatric to emotional to physical) can seek remedy for their afflictions in the barnyard. Patients are placed in an environment where interaction with farm animals constitutes an integral part of the therapy. Activities include feeding, milking, cleaning out stalls, and other types of "chores." These places will back up their assertion with research showing that such pastimes have a therapeutic effect on many patients. Conditions that fall under this broad banner include psychosis, neurosis, anxiety, depression, behavior disorders, addiction, and even dementia.

The field has been growing and is sometimes referred to as "care farming." Here vulnerable groups of people (whether for health, social, or educational reasons) engage in farming practices as part of a structured program under careful supervision. Individuals work with animals, crops, gardens, etc. In some programs, kids with social, emotional, behavioral, and learning challenges are exposed to the farm environment and participate in various activities. They have buildings with names like "The Teaching Barn" where enrolled students learn to care for livestock. The program is designed to foster the development of life skills such as discipline and confidence.

Psychologists have recently identified a syndrome that they refer to as "nature deficit disorder." The basic premise is that children who spend too much time indoors and out of touch with nature have a higher tendency to develop behavior disorders. In my day, if you were beyond conventional remedies, you got sent to a place called reform school. This modern version, I suppose, is re*farm* school. Farms for f@^ked-up kids, they are sometimes called. Many psychologists and researchers endorse the idea that an individual receives help by becoming a helper. There are course curriculums laid out for various levels and needs. At two campuses in New York State there is an admissions process that includes a referral from an eligible school district.

Movie Theatres That Used to Be Barns

The Old Barn Theater is part of Parry Lodge, a resort in Utah that's almost a hundred years old. The barn used to be a stable where famous horses were kept, including Roy Roger's "Trigger," the Lone Ranger's "Silver," and Tonto's "Scout." The barn was repurposed as a bucolic western theater and regularly runs films originally shot in the area.

The Barn Cinema can be found at Dartington Hall, a scenic fourteenth-century estate in Devon, England. The barn began operating as a cinema in the nineteen-seventies and was renovated again in the late nineties. After-theatre libations are available at the estate's gastropub, The White Hart, a short walk from the barn.

The Barn Theater in Frenchtown, New Jersey was open until about the mid-nineteen-eighties and the last movie featured was *The Abyss*. It has since been converted into an office complex. Because of its cavernous construction it wasn't uncommon for patrons to experience an echo from the soundtrack during a showing.

CHAPTER EIGHT

Out Behind the Barn

I was so naïve as a kid I used to sneak out
behind the barn and do nothing.
JOHNNY CARSON

True Confessions

At one time the barn served as a place where you could go to get away from watchful eyes and do the things you might not try elsewhere. Certainly in my childhood we went there to smoke the cigarettes we'd purchased from Mr. Reimer at the general store under false pretences (usually by saying we had been sent by one adult or another to buy them). We smashed and ate the watermelons we'd stolen out of the neighbour's garden, read magazines we thought would be disapproved of.

There's a litany of illicit activity associated with the idea of taking oneself—in both the literal and figurative sense—"out behind the barn," first kisses and stolen liquor and a general leaning toward the licentious. There have been songs written about it, like the one Little Jimmy Dickens used to sing. "I got my education out behind the barn..." he intones, and goes on to list assortment of "lessons," but also sings that it was the place where, "my pappy used to tan my hide," something that could also be accomplished out behind the woodshed.

In a child's first awkward attempts to escape the confines of the farmhouse, to break free of continual surveillance, the first stage might be a visit to the barnyard, away from the prying eyes but still within the circle of familiarity. It was a place where you could try something new, possibly sinful. I have no doubt the idea of sin still holds a place in the mind of a twenty-first century child, but in many cases it has surely been modified and transfigured into something other than disobedience to the credo of an angry god. The twenty-first century equivalent might be a secret visit to a forbidden website.

When I was out behind the barn looking at stolen copies of my mother's *True Confessions* magazines for pictures of women in states of partial undress, I had no illusions about the hard truth my Sunday School lessons had taught me: that the god of wrath and vengeance was right there with me, but I was prepared to deal with that—it was the parents that posed a larger problem. The Almighty could be taken care of with a simple prayer of repentance, but the disapproving mother would not be so easy to appease. I considered it a kind of staging area for the foolish risks I would take later in adolescence. I could still run into the house and clutch my mother's skirt at a moment's notice if I needed to, and I could still come if I was called, but I was not under observation.

It was not the most romantic of places, for it was likely to be not far from discarded and rotting bales of hay, feed gone bad, derelict machinery, and quite possibly a manure pile. But the whole idea was that it was a place where you were out of sight. Of course, it didn't always have to be outside the barn. There was a lot that could happen inside the barn as well, in various locations, not the least of which would be the hayloft.

The idea that a farmer watches over his animals, as the shepherd over his flock, is an interesting one. When there's a barn to herd them into they are well looked after, but in the absence of one, there's need for a shepherd. The second generation of the human race, according to the Bible, saw Abel choose a life as a semi-nomadic herdsman. Cain,

Building Of The Ark by Bedford Master. The scene depicted here bears a remarkable resemblance to a pioneer barn raising! FROM THE *BEDFORD BOOK OF HOURS*, 1423. BRITISH MUSEUM, LONDON. VIA WIKIMEDIA COMMONS

on the other hand, took to farming and tilled the soil. Some argue that the root of the conflict between them stemmed from the fact that one chose farming and the other sheepherding as a profession. Others make the case that Moses was favoured by God because of his gentle way with animals. King David, of course, herded sheep and camels, and Jacob's family problems began when he refused to take up shepherding. Even Abraham, the man at the root of the world's major religions (Islam, Christianity, Judaism) was a shepherd, and Jesus himself is referred to as Agnus Dei, the Lamb of God.

Oh, Behave

When it comes to surveillance, there's a whole field of psychology that examines the notion of being watched. Some of these studies test whether human beings can detect when they are being stared at, a psychic effect known by the technical term of *scopaesthesia*. The jury is out, but some people swear by it and the concept persists in the field of parapsychology. Real or imagined, countless experiments have been developed with children and adults alike to see how they behave when they don't think they are being watched. The researcher steps out of the room and the one-way mirror or the camera records what happens next. There are even studies that have come to the conclusion that the idea of being watched can make you a better person. According to *Scientific American*, a recent field study involved experiments in which posters depicting the faces of people with eyes staring out at the viewer were hung up on the walls of a busy cafeteria. The effect brought about a significant improvement in the cleanliness of the place, and the explanation was that the sense of being observed caused more people to feel the impetus to clean up after themselves.

The idea that we behave differently when we think we are being watched has significant implications in a world where we are constantly being monitored—with or without our knowledge—by means of the electronic gadgetry we are in constant interaction with. If you are an active participant in social media, you are in fact under a constant state of scrutiny by all those millions of others out there, not to mention the makers of the software itself. You are part of a vast "herd," and you are being shepherded by the likes of Mark Zuckerberg and his minions.

The idea of being watched can be taken too far in some individuals, who develop a condition known as *scopophobia*. It can get so bad that these people will not even deign to step out of their houses or apartments, so profound is their discomfort. There are also phobias associated with the barn. *Equinophobia*, also known as *hippophobia,* is an irrational fear of horses. People with *fundophobia* fear farms in general. Sufferers list specifics such as being afraid that they will be subjected to "stinking smells," injury by animals, or an obsessive fear that they will be crushed by a falling silo. *Haraphobiai* involves fear of pigsties.

Botanophobia refers to fear of plants. This fear seems to center around the idea that they will evolve someday to the point where they develop the ability to eat people. *Bovinophobia*, also known as *tauro-phobia,* is fear of cows. Not only can these folks not even be around the animals, they can't even stand to think about them. Even seeing a cow on TV can set off an attack.

Swinophobia is fear of pigs, and needless to say these individuals rarely if ever eat pork. *Alektorophobia* is a deathly fear of chickens, and *Ornithophobia* is fear of owls. *Ovinophobia* is fear of sheep, and *Lachanophobia* is fear of vegetables. *Mechanophobia* is fear of machinery.

And of course there are people who suffer from fear of barns themselves, but I haven't been able to find a proper name for that as of yet.

"Curiouser and Curiouser"

If the idea of being watched really does have an effect on human behavior there are plenty of implications that arise from it, certainly in the field of morality, but what happens when we take the idea back to the place we started from—the barnyard? What about the animals themselves? Looking a wild creature in the eye can have a disconcerting effect. Most of them view eye contact as a threat. On the other hand, domestic animals often seem oblivious to it. The one exception is the dog, which is about the only animal on a farm that you can make eye contact with.

There has been some literature on this subject as well. In the realm of non-fiction, Rosamund Young has written *The Secret Life of Cows,* in which she documents how cows and pigs and hens play elaborate games, sulk, hold grudges, and exhibit all manner of behavior from peer pressure to romantic overtures that we normally associate only with our own species.

A plethora of stories have been written that depict animals in the barn as entirely different when there are no bothersome humans around to watch them. And it isn't just allegory, as in George Orwell's *Animal Farm*; in stories like *Charlotte's Web* and *Babe* the barnyard creatures hide their true nature from their human keepers. It requires a huge suspension of disbelief to go along with notion that animals possess higher levels of cognitive functioning and language, but could there be a grain of truth to this idea? Does animal behaviour change in any appreciable manner when they sense they are being observed by us? If so, it speaks to the notion that they may indeed know when they are being watched.

Then there's the matter of their exceptional senses. My dog, Eddy, used to like to lie on the bed in the room down the hall while I was at work in my study. I couldn't see him, and he couldn't see me. But it was just impossible to sneak up on him. As quietly as I made my way over to the bedroom, as furtively as I poked my head around the doorway, by the time my eyes fell on him he had already raised his head and perked up his ears in response to my detected proximity. It happened without fail. What tipped him off to my approach?

The idea that observation can affect behavior applies not just to the animal world. Even subatomic particles exhibit this phenomenon. Quantum physicists have ascertained that electrons behave one way when they are being observed and quite a different way when they are not, as demonstrated by one of the most famous experiments in the history of scientific discovery: the double-slit experiment. In this test, electrons are beamed at a barrier into which a pair of slits have been cut, allowing some of the electrons to pass through and strike a photoelectric screen, where they show up as little dots of light. The expected result is that two bands of light will form on the screen, each corresponding to the opening in the barrier. Instead, a very different pattern forms, one that exactly resembles what happens when *waves*, not particles pass through.

Particles behaving as if they were waves is strange enough, but this is where things get, as Alice might say, "curiouser and curiouser." When a detection device is attached at the site of entry into each slot, so that the electrons can be "observed" as they pass through, the pattern that forms on the screen behind the barrier abruptly changes. Now two bright bands form, just as they would if *particles* were passing through the slits. And then, as soon as the "observer" is withdrawn, the pattern reverts back to a series of light and dark bands produced by the action of waves. It's as if the electrons know when they are being watched, and "change their minds" accordingly, deciding to act one way rather than another, depending on the situation. They seem to have a will of their own. It is one of the truly baffling aspects of subatomic physics and incontrovertible proof that, at least at the level of very small entities, the mere act of observation affects behavior.

Maybe the same goes for cows and chickens. And as for humans, we've added a nice touch by bringing religion into the mix, which includes the idea of never truly being alone, for God (whichever version of that deity you choose to invoke) is always with us, always watching (over) us. "*His eye is on the sparrow, and I know he watches me.*" Even if you're a non-believer there's still the matter of your conscience, which in a sense constantly "oversees" your every thought and action. This may explain why as humans we almost never feel truly "free," unlike Friedrich Nietzsche's "Ubermensch," who stands alone in unfettered liberation because he has unshackled himself from the chains of all moral imperatives but his own. "Man is a rope," Nietzsche offers, "that's fastened between animal and Ubermensch—a rope over an abyss." The word *Ubermensch* literally translates as "above man," i.e. someone who transcends the notion of paying homage to an "overseer," and who lives outside the limits of any imposed moral code but the one entirely of his own creation.

But do those cows and chickens and horses in the barn have a moral code of their own, some sort of crude array of imperatives they feel obliged to follow? Consider the pigeons that populate our inner cities. They are direct descendants of what is probably the oldest domesticated animal in the world, the rock dove. Studies have determined that they have a rigid code of conduct when it comes to eating the breadcrumbs and seeds that are scattered before them. Whatever the number of pigeons present, they will divide the supply in such a way as to ensure that every bird gets approximately the same amount of food. It's a fairly complex behavioral pattern that's also very reliable and repeats itself time and again. But is it driven by moral considerations? Or does it amount to some sort of Darwinian survival technique? This may not be much of a question until you consider that our *own* moral behavior may be driven by Darwinian models as well, i.e., human morality as a direct product of evolution.

Perhaps a more compelling question is whether we owe the animals themselves any moral consideration. Someone who goes into a building and opens fire on the crowd below certainly doesn't think he owes anyone down there any sympathies in that regard. But what about someone who slaughters animals for their meat? Or the person who eats that meat? Should I be having second thoughts about the pig who supplied the bacon I fried in my pan this morning?

A Darker Side

The big turkey barn we had dismantled and rebuilt in its new location now stood much closer to the farmyard than before. There was a fence to keep the birds enclosed, but when a few birds managed to escape, as they inevitably did, they would wander through the yard and head straight for my mother's garden. The dog was encouraged to give chase immediately, lest the peas and beans and radishes didn't make it to the dinner table. There wasn't any harm in it until one day, instead of merely scattering them, the dog suddenly launched itself through the air, dug its paws into the broad back of a sprinting

The big turkey barn. It's part of a Christmas tree farm now, and a portion of the cavernous interior has been converted into a winter wonderland for children. AUTHOR PHOTO

bird, opened its jaws and snapped the bird's neck with one quick bite. The turkey crashed to the ground, flailed, and flapped its wings in a death spiral, while the dog ran around in circles barking gleefully. I thought it might be a one-time occurrence, but something had been triggered, and when the next unfortunate gaggle of turkeys wandered into the yard the same scenario was repeated. When my father found out, I was immediately ordered to put the dog down.

I was allowed to use the .22 caliber single-shot rifle for the job. The .303 bolt action would have been the better choice, but the bullets for that gun were too expensive. Remember this was the same man who, at hog slaughtering time, would not bother to waste ammunition on a pig, and chose to use a sledgehammer instead. I can still picture the uncanny way he had of mesmerizing the doomed hog as he stood before it and then, *wham!* Time for the butcher knife.

Besides the small and disappointing house our father had moved us into, the farmyard we now called home also had a couple of traditional barns. One was an ancient relic that must have been put up by the first settlers. Built out of rough-hewn logs and plaster, it sagged badly, and we had filled it up with the detritus of turkey ranching: brooders and feeders, watering troughs and rolls of fencing wire. The other one was newer, red of course, and in better condition. It was going to serve as a repository for the grain needed to feed the turkeys. I chose the backside of this newer barn, and the dog followed me dutifully when I called it, stood before me, looking up at me with eager eyes, wondering what sport I might have in mind for the two of us. It waited with its eyes of innocent curiosity. Were we going to go on a hunt together? Did I have some hidden treat I was about to share? I raised the rifle, aimed between its eyes, and fired. The dog went down and I walked quickly over to the toolshed to put down the gun and exchange it for a spade, then started back to give the dog a decent burial. When I rounded the corner of the barn it was standing there looking up at me, confused and badly wounded, blood running down its snout. The small bullet had failed to penetrate its skull. I ran back for the gun and this time fired again, then again, at the same spot until I was sure the damage had been done.

Do I have an accurate memory as to my state of mind? Could I have taken the dog to a distant farm and pleaded with the people there to look after it? I would have had to tell them it had tasted blood. It wasn't as though I hadn't shot and killed other animals by then—owls and cats and badgers and many kinds of vermin. As horrifying as that may be to today's highly sensitive urban dwellers, it was part of life on the farm. It didn't matter how much I hated to carry out the deed. It was either shoot the dog or face harsh consequences: humiliation, threats, shouting, physical force—all from a man I loved above all others. I put away the gun, hooked the tractor up to the stone boat, and hauled the body away to bury it.

Why did I do all this out behind the barn? Because I didn't want my mother to see. She spent a lot of time at the kitchen counter and I knew that from there, even as small in stature as she was, there was a chance she would look out through the window and see what I was up to. I wanted to spare her that, and spare myself the extra pain. I was thankful that she hadn't seen me botch the whole thing, although she might have heard the first shot and looked out to see me running back for the rifle a second time, heard the subsequent shots and figured it all out. I never asked, and she never brought it up.

The interior of this barn has been left bare to showcase the mortise and tenon construction of its beams and timbers, planks and trusses. AUTHOR SKETCH

CHAPTER NINE

Who Said Size Doesn't Matter?

*There were beams across the second story, supporting
poles on which the hay was piled. What great haymows
they were, choice romping places for children!*
GERTRUDE LEFFERTS VANDERBILT

Things Go Viral

If huge sprawling barns make the practice of animal husbandry more efficient and productive these improvements don't come without a price. One of the problems with big barns where so many animals are raised in close proximity is that disease can spread quickly with devastating results. An intensive poultry operation where birds are crowded together in dry and dusty conditions is an ideal place for a viral outbreak. But there is also a genetic factor. The animals are bred for faster growth rates and higher meat yields, sometimes for higher rates of egg or milk production, and to accomplish that little room is left for genetic variation. Diversity is the enemy. Uniformity is the desired outcome of any breeding strategy, and ideally, every turkey and chicken should be identical to every other so that when the final product reaches the store shelf the quality control is so high that every T-bone steak looks every other T-bone steak, every pot roast and broiler chicken is interchangeable with every other.

A few of the more common diseases that can affect a flock of chickens include Aspergillosis, Avian Influenza, Histomoniasis, Botulism, Campylobacteriosis, Coccidiosis, Erysipelas, Fatty Liver Hemorrhagic Syndrome, Fowl Cholera, Fowlpox, Fowl Typhoid, Gallid Herpesvirus, Gapeworm, Infectious Bronchitis, Infectious Bursal Disease, Marek's Disease, Psittacosis, Pullorum, Squamous Cell Carcinoma, Tibial Dyschondroplasia, Toxoplasmosis, and Ulcerative Enteritis.

Breeding for genetic uniformity also brings about another side effect: the animals become more susceptible to disease because their immune systems become increasingly compromised. A new virus can spread with alarming speed and efficiency. And when a virus makes the leap to another species as sometimes happens, a disease like Covid-19 or Avian flu becomes a threat not only to the animals but to the humans who come into contact with them.

What Goes Around Comes Around

Overcrowding and genetic breeding can make domestic animals more susceptible to disease, but it can also make them less intelligent. The job of feeding all those turkeys fell to my grandfather and me and we'd start as soon as I got home from school. Just as in the former place, the traditional barn had been converted into a granary, gutted and cleaned up to be used for feed storage, and we'd spend hour upon hour in there throwing buckets of wheat and oats and various supplements into a hammer mill to be shredded. Then it was shot into a big mixer my father had welded together that was large enough to process six tons of grain at a go.

When the mixer was full, we'd use a tractor to haul it out to the turkey barn and fill up the feeders there. The turkeys would gather in huge flocks to follow the proceedings, and we would have to go slow to keep from running them over. As soon as we stopped, they would surround the mixer entirely, and it happened sometimes that some rogue bits of grain would fall onto a metal ledge that ran along the back of the mixer. These morsels looked very inviting to the birds, but to get at it they had to stick their necks out, literally, and risk getting caught up in the gigantic chain that turned upon an enormous sprocket there. The unfortunate bird would get hoisted up into air and carried around the full circumference of the wheel, only to fall back to the ground with its neck all but severed. It was an arresting sight, but the learning curve for the avian bystanders was practically zero. The rest of the flock would disperse momentarily and in short order go right back to pecking at the bits of grain falling onto the ledge. I think we must have welded some sort of shield into place to keep it from happening, but the truth is I can't remember.

Better Never Than Late

Near the end of one growing season we had an alarming outbreak of disease, and because so many birds were dying, my father insisted they should be collected and stored until he could choose a few samples to take to Winnipeg, where the animal scientists at the University of Manitoba would examine them in order to determine what was killing them. I knew it was a bad idea to leave them there for long, but I was forbidden from hauling them off, and when the weather turned cold and ground froze, still they lay piled up inside the barn. They were forgotten over the course of the winter until spring brought an early wave of warm weather that thawed the birds out and left me to deal with the mess.

I knew it was going to be bad even before I pulled the stone boat up to the entrance and forced myself to open the door of the shed. The stench was unearthly, but I felt relieved to discover that the pile of dead turkeys appeared to have survived relatively intact. It wasn't until I went to get hold of one and the turkey's leg came away from the rest of carcass effortlessly that I suspected things might be worse than I'd feared. I'd brought the pitchfork with me for just this eventuality and now I thrust it into the pile and made the mistake of moving things around. The entire mass suddenly came alive, and as I lifted the fork away thousands of maggots rained down out of it. With each fork-ful they fell like rice from the carrion, which had disintegrated and putrefied to such a degree that forking it up became all but impossible.

Worse, in disturbing the rotting mass the smell became greatly intensified. I fought to keep from throwing up. My only salvation rested in a brisk southerly wind that often accompanied such early warm weather. It allowed me to effect a strategy where I took a few steps upwind, inhaled deeply, ran back to plunge the pitchfork into the writhing mass, threw the carrion onto the stone boat (still holding my breath), and then stepped back upwind, lungs bursting, to take in a fresh supply of air. It went on for a very long time, and I made many trips to "feather hill."

Between a Rock and a Hard Place

Hauling the dead turkeys on the stone boat for burial was the easy part, digging the hole to throw them into would prove a greater challenge. The poor rocky soil we had rebuilt the turkey barn on proved to have some unique features because it marked the shoreline of an ancient inland sea. You'd only dig a foot or so before your spade struck a layer of material that was all but impenetrable, a tightly compacted aggregate of stone and gravel that you had to hack through with great effort. Thankfully, this layer was only about six inches thick, and once you got through it there was nothing but pure white sand that you could carve through like butter. But you had to be careful. The hole could cave in on you at the slightest disturbance, and if you had made the mistake of digging too close to an old grave, the resulting cave-in would see decomposed turkeys, with all the attendant odours and putrefaction, spilling into the hole you had just dug.

The Expendables

On the family farm of the recent past, when Betsy the milk cow dried up, it was a big deal. She would have been remembered as a creature who gave much goodness and sustenance to the family, and her fate would have been a matter for careful consideration. A decision would have been made as to whether she should merely be put out to pasture or slaughtered for meat. If she had died suddenly of unknown causes, there would have been the matter of what to do with the carcass.

In a large modern dairy operation, things are different. The cows are impregnated every year, using artificial insemination, to get them to lactate. When the calf is born it's immediately and perfunctorily taken away, notwithstanding the considerable suffering and stress this causes both mother and calf. If the calf happens to be the wrong sex, i.e. male, it's off to the feedlot to be raised for veal or other meat, while the females are raised to replace the older cows when they no longer produce enough milk.

Thanks to the use of drugs and hormones and other techniques, the cows are able to meet staggering levels of milk production unattainable in the past. Their bodies are coaxed to produce as much as four times the amount of milk they would have only fifty years ago, but it's difficult for them to keep it up for very long. The normal lifespan of a cow is about twenty years, but dairy cows only live for about five. By that age, the intensive regimen of twice daily milking, constant standing on concrete floors, repeated impregnation, and the general wear and tear of being kept in production constantly without rest, has left them spent.

The average dairy cow produces about twenty thousand pounds of milk in a single year and once production falls below fifteen litres per day or so, the writing is on the wall. A slaughtered dairy cow's meat is used for low grade burgers and processed meat production rather than being sold as cuts of beef, or it might be sent off to the abattoir. If you happen to be a male bovine and are lucky enough to get chosen to be raised as a veal calf, you will be slaughtered well before your first birthday. If you're raised for regular beef you generally don't make it through your second. And even if you're lucky enough to become a breeding bull, chances are you'll still be gone by your third birthday.

The prospects of a normal existence for other domesticated animals these days is equally grim, and most can expect to be around for a much shorter time than their natural life expectancy. Pigs can live for about ten or twelve years but are usually slaughtered by the time they reach five or six months. It's the same story for sheep and turkeys, which would otherwise enjoy about the same length of time on Earth as hogs. Other farm animals live even shorter lives. Broiler chickens, for instance, are gone in six weeks, but perhaps the most unfortunate of all are the male chicks hatched in operations devoted to egg production. Good for nothing, they are generally dispatched within a day. The baby chicks are "sexed" immediately after hatching, and some operations have a high-speed grinder on site into which the males are simply tossed for quick disposal. Less efficient operations use another method known as "cervical dislocation," which is a fancy way of saying they get their necks wrung.

Those Ornery Varmints

Creatures great and small have been attracted to barns for as long as they've been in existence. What could be more natural than wanting to hang out in a place where food is obtainable with a minimum of effort? Skunks, raccoons, mice, rabbits, rats, snakes, weasels, groundhogs, voles, coyotes, badgers, stoats, hedgehogs, and other animals are a constant problem when they invade the barnyard and have generally become known as vermin. In the early days when barns were smaller, the way to deal with this problem was to keep a predator or two around, perhaps a barn cat or a rat terrier. Then there are all the bothersome insects: flies, ticks, fleas, mites, lice beetles, ants, and gnats to name a few. Early ways of dealing with the problem included poison, and of course, good old DDT. We used plenty of it on our farm. I was often sent into the barn or summer kitchen clutching a spray pump filled with the deadly chemical to kill anything that came into contact with it, except of course me, though I inhaled a goodly amount of the stuff.

One of the original manual sprayers (a hand pump with a plunger at one end and a little tank at the other) was known as the FLIT. It used mineral oil and DDT produced by the Standard Oil Company of New Jersey, which later became Esso, and then Exxon. Pest control executive Robert Loibl, along with his wife, ingested DDT on a regular basis to prove that it was harmless. They even partook of a drink called a Mickey Slim that had DDT as one of the ingredients. The chemical was marketed by a subsidiary called Stanco, which ran an extensive ad campaign. The artwork for the long-running campaign was developed by Theodore Seuss Geisel, at the time not yet the successful author of so many beloved children's books. His ads depicted scenes of recreational and domestic activities being interrupted by oversized, whimsical flying creatures menacing people with their stingers. They often featured the caption, "Quick, Henry. The FLIT!" The animals and creatures Seuss drew for these ads are instantly recognizable as the work of the man who would later create *The Cat in the Hat* and *Green Eggs and Ham*. The vintage metal bug sprayers still sell on eBay for considerable sums. They have names like *Chapin, Fly Toy, Hudson, Black Flag, Zephyr,* and *White Rose.*

Pests Aside

When smaller barns gave way to the large-scale farming operations of today, a couple of cats and a scrappy terrier weren't going to cut it any longer, and so the advent of a huge industry sprang up. The chemical production of insecticides, herbicides, fungicides, etc. became big business, and companies like Monsanto and Dow Chemical were on the leading edge, forging ahead with the production of many types of pesticides.

The Food and Agriculture Organization (FAO) defines pesticide as any substance designed for the prevention, destruction, or control of pests, such as undesirable species of plants or animals that impede the growth, processing, storage, etc. of agricultural commodities. This includes defoliants, desiccants, and other agents. That covers a lot of ground. Monsanto had already made massive profits from the production of large quantities of Agent Orange, the deadly chemical used in the Vietnam War to defoliate the Asian jungle and make it easier to spot those pesky Viet Cong lurking under all that cover. These days Monsanto is working hard to position itself as a positive force working to mitigate climate change. Their website emphasizes the efficiency of their pesticide products, which translates into fewer passes over the crops to spray them, which means reduced greenhouse gas emissions.

CHAPTER TEN

Don't Fence Me In

I found a fine place to read and pray, on the top floor of that barn building where the rabbits used to be—as soon as I am alone and silent again, I sink into deep peace, recollection, and happiness.
THOMAS MERTON READER

Why Me?

Old Macdonald's Farm isn't populated by just any group of creatures. The animals that have become associated with the barnyard amount to an exclusive club. But how did it come about that the verses in the song are about pigs and cows and sheep. Why not zebras and tapirs and vicunas instead? There are plenty of other animals to choose from, after all. Why, for example, has the bison never been domesticated to the extent that the cow has? And then there are all the various kinds of deer out there. They seem like good candidates for domestication. Why, with the exception of the reindeer, do they remain largely untamed? The vicuna of South America produces some of the finest wool in the world, but the animal remains in the wild. What are the chances things might have turned out differently?

There are good reasons why the mounted soldier in years past didn't ride a rhinoceros into battle instead of a horse. The fact of the

Childhood dream of a barn AUTHOR WATERCOLOUR

matter is that the particular breeds of horses and chickens and goats we see today are the result of a great deal of trial and error. There's hardly an animal out there that someone hasn't tried to domesticate at one time or another, but all too often these attempts have failed for reasons that come down a few basic considerations. A lot of the time it comes down to chemicals. Cortisol, for instance, is a stress hormone found in animals (as well as humans) to a greater or lesser extent, depending on the species. Creatures that produce smaller amounts of it tend to be less skittish and not startled as easily, which makes them better candidates for taming.

Other things to consider include territorial behavior, and fight or flight reflexes. Then there's sociability. Some animals just seem naturally ornery and bad-tempered. Those who tend to be loners aren't a good bet compared to those who prefer to live in groups, where the hierarchy of a social order makes them more predictable and easier to handle. Some animals have a natural inbred trait toward submissiveness which can be transferred from animals to humans that makes them easier to work with. A barnyard where everyone knows their place is a happy barnyard.

One of the biggest obstacles often turns out to be reproduction. Getting animals to breed in captivity can be a challenge. We've already learned how some animals seem more sensitive to being kept or watched than others, and some species simply refuse to engage in reproductive activity (whether mothering or mating) under such circumstances. And just as there are certain animals a lot of us don't want to be around, spiders and snakes for example, some animals clearly disdain the company of humans and would just as soon not have anything to do with us.

Others are just plain deadly. It wouldn't make much sense to populate the barn with timber wolves and grizzly bears, but it's important to remember that even the relatively docile animals we see today were wild once. Their behavior is not entirely predictable, and none of them have a perfect track record. More than one farmer has suffered an unfortunate heart attack while tending the hogs and been found partially eaten. In one particularly gruesome incident, all that remained behind was a set of false teeth. In another case, a set of young parents working out in the barnyard came upon the pigs chewing on their son's head. Apparently the toddler had crawled into the pen where he was set upon by hungry hogs.

Farmers have been trampled by cows, kicked by horses, butted by goats, bitten by pigs, horned by bulls, and pecked by poultry. My mother liked to tell of the time she took me out to the turkey barn one morning after my father, being an idea man, had foisted yet another chore upon her, even though she already had a thousand and one things to do back at the house. She was soon busy with her task and left me unattended for a few moments. I became an object of interest to some of the nearby turkey toms, large and aggressive male birds that you see in photos with their wings furled out, tails fanned wide, chest feathers puffed and necks craned back. They do that when they are about to hurt you.

Upon completion of her chores—which were in fact *not* her chores at all—my mother discovered that I had come under siege from the avian equivalent of a gang of thugs. By the time she reached me I had been thrown to the ground, pecked and clawed and scratched, and was lying curled up in a fetal position, hands over my face to keep them from plucking my eyes out. My mother fought her way through the angry and fowl mob, vanquished the horde of attackers, and spirited me off to safety. I have no memory of this, but my mother always got a big kick out of telling that story. I think it was because she was the hero of it. It wasn't often she found reason to characterize herself that way, and it is one of my great regrets that I never told her when she was alive that it was she, and not my father, I'd always thought of as my hero.

Domestication should be distinguished from taming. Almost any animal can be tamed at certain times under certain circumstances. Take the wolf. If raised from birth it can be quite tame, but when it reaches a certain age it will simply refuse to behave the way a dog does and will attempt to revert to "wild" ways. Often, animals are taken out of the wild and raised in captivity. It's not unusual in some parts of the world for animals to be captured in the jungle as babies, raised as pets, and eaten when they reach adulthood. I've witnessed this firsthand in the villages of the Yucatan Peninsula, where children could be seen cuddling anteaters on leashes and playing with them like pets. When I made further enquiries, I was a little taken aback to learn of their pet's ultimate fate. And yet, how do I reconcile that with the knowledge of what happens to those cute little chicks in the petting zoo when they lose their downy feathers and become chickens?

Another Kind of Barn

My very first teaching assignment was a position in a fancy new school that had not yet been stocked with any textbooks or supplies to speak of. I was hired as a science specialist and it would be my job to teach students from grades one to six. I had nothing to work with, so I decided to make use of the empty terrariums that had been built into the open area where I would hold my classes. I got hold of an incubator and some fertilized eggs, and started up a project to hatch some chicks. The students would learn about embryo development and such, and when the chicks hatched, we would raise them inside the state-of-the-art glass enclosures, which happened to be climate controlled.

The project was highly successful, and we soon had a terrarium full of squawking young chickens that needed regular feeding and watering. Growth charts were drawn up, careful observations were made and records kept, but of course the birds also made a hell of a mess, which didn't please the janitor at all, and things only got worse when the birds grew big enough for the students to take outside for recess, where they proceeded to scatter their droppings all over the pavement and other areas of the playground. We really got into the nutritional science of the thing though, implementing a feeding regimen that saw half the chicks raised on a diet of store-bought chick starter while the other half were fed a special diet developed by the students that consisted mostly of ground-up wheat along with some supplements. The results were spectacular. The nutritionists working for the commercial feed companies had certainly done their homework, because the birds on that diet weighed at least twice as much as the ones raised on our home-grown product.

But then came the end of the school year, by which time some of the students had become very attached to the chickens, and it was hard to see them go, even though we had found a new home for them on a farm near the city. In addition to driving the janitor up the wall, we probably broke every health rule in the book. I doubt I'd get away with anything like that now, but it sure was fun. I like to think those kids learned more science that year then any textbook could have taught them.

During the next term, we decided to try tadpole farming, which also turned out to be a very useful teaching opportunity that led to other projects, including crayfish farming and rabbit farming. We even managed a single-celled animal farm, which required the loan of a class set of microscopes from the nearby high school. There were some spectacular, and in fairness, some tragic results (the tadpoles suffered a mysterious mass extinction) but altogether that terrarium/barn served a very useful purpose. Years later, I would be stopped on a busy city street by a former student from one of those classes who recognized me. He wanted to let me know that he was doing important scientific work now, and that he'd never forgotten the thrill of looking through the microscope at all those little wiggling parameciums and amoebas in grade school, and it was that experience that had inspired him to take up the study of microbiology.

Hit and Miss

Merely capturing a wild species of animal and keeping it in captivity doesn't meet the threshold of domestication, so some animals are considered semi-domesticated. The Asian elephant, for instance, is not bred in captivity but rather the young are captured in the wild and raised to be tame. Then there's the farm in Russia where they've been trying to breed foxes in captivity for some time, with limited success. Other semi-domesticated creatures include American bison, elk, muskox, and emu. Crocodiles, a species that has existed since the time of dinosaurs, are farmed extensively in some parts of Louisiana for meat, leather, and other products. Cajun cuisine often calls for alligator meat. *The Alligator Gourmet Cookbook* is an entire volume dedicated to preparing dishes using this meat. They're also farmed in places like Israel, Australia, and Cambodia. The Nile crocodile is farmed all over the African continent, and in some places they are skinned alive to make handbags. But in none of these cases are the animals truly considered tame, in the sense that you can handle them the way you would cows or sheep.

The list of failed attempts at domestication is long and filled with surprising twists and turns. In North America you can drive through the Central Plains and see the skeletal remains of the abandoned barns left behind by these doomed operations. One of the most spectacular failures was the craze of chinchilla farming that was going to make so many farmers rich. Chinchillas were touted as docile animals that were easy to house, inexpensive to raise, and highly profitable when sold for their fur. They are rodents, somewhat larger than a ground squirrel and native to the Andes of South America, where at one time they thrived in great numbers in a collective arrangement somewhere between a colony and a herd. Their pelts were indeed considered of some value as they produced a soft, durable fur. Notwithstanding their desirability, it took about a hundred and fifty of the little critters to make a decent coat. By the turn of the twentieth century they had been hunted pretty much into extinction in their native environment, but about a dozen or so were brought up to the United States in the twenties and bred successfully in captivity.

By the nineteen-fifties something of a craze had taken hold in many parts of North America as scams sprang up to breed and sell baby chinchillas. Huge profits were promised to prospective ranchers as part of a "get-rich-quick" scheme that convinced them they need only raise the animals to adulthood in hastily constructed barns and the money would come pouring in. But some unforeseen challenges soon emerged. To begin with, because chinchillas are essentially mountain creatures best suited to a temperate climate and lack the ability to sweat, unless a rancher was prepared to undertake the prohibitive expense of air conditioning his barn, the chinchillas were going to suffer greatly. When the hot weather arrived, heat stroke killed them by the thousands.

It also turned out that as the chinchillas grew older, they became susceptible to a variety of factious diseases, not to mention that they had very sensitive gastrointestinal systems and were constantly swinging between constipation and diarrhea. And then there was the matter of their much-needed dust baths, which had been an integral part of their regimen in the wild. A lot of animals take them regularly to remove parasites and excess oils, loosen substrate material, and a host of other reasons. They're essential for clean healthy skin and a well-groomed coat of feathers or fur. There's also the fact that a chinchilla, just like its cousin the beaver, has teeth that grow continually and need to be worn down. Of course none of this information was featured in the ads that sprang up all over the continent in the fifties and so the chinchilla farms failed one after another. Most operators gave up after a year or two, and the abandoned chinchilla barns still remain here and there as a requiem to their folly.

There were plenty of other flops as well, including an attempt by the pre-civil war American army to use camels as pack animals. As so often happens with such cases, some of the animals managed to escape into the wild, but the herd didn't thrive and soon died off. They did much better in Australia where they were domesticated in large numbers at one time, and where the population of feral camels today is close to three quarters of a million. Water buffalo released into the wild have done well there, too, as have herds of feral sheep in Scotland.

The extreme example of the feral animal is the dingo dog of Australia, which has officially been placed into the category of a wild—and not feral—animal. They were originally domestic dogs that had accompanied their masters as they travelled out of Southeast Asia into Australia many thousands of years ago. A burial site recently unearthed in the Middle East shows that foxes in that part of the world may have been part of a failed attempt at domestication at one time. The site dates back to sixteen thousand years ago (which pre-dates the domestication of dogs).

The pigeons we see so prominently in the cities were originally domesticated birds bred from the wild rock dove that subsequently became feral. The dove's natural habitat consisted of sea cliffs and mountains, which may explain why pigeons seem to be so at home along the ledges and roofs of multi-storey urban office buildings today.

In some parts of the world, the reindeer, buffalo, yak, camel, llama, and alpaca have been domesticated.

The domestication of large land animals served as a catalyst for major advancements in many civilizations. Consider that without the labour of horse and oxen, the cultivation of untamed land in North America would never have been possible. Without pigs and cattle and chickens as a source of food, without sheep as source of wool for warm clothing, the pioneers simply could not have survived, never mind accomplish what they did. Now we have the luxury of becoming vegetarians and wearing only non-organic clothing, but it wasn't always so.

It's safe to say that some barnyard creatures would not likely survive in the wild, sheep for instance, which must be shorn in the summer or they will die of heatstroke. On the other hand, pigs become an absolute scourge when they go feral. Some creatures seem to fall in between—the leaf-cutter alfalfa bee for instance—where arguments exist on both sides as to whether they have truly been domesticated. What are those little buildings constructed for them if not barns, the ones you see spread out across an alfalfa field, all with open doors facing the same direction, there for them to nest in? And what do the bees construct their nests out of? Why, alfalfa leaves, of course. In the process of gathering them, they rub against the purple and yellow flowers, which need to be pollinated if they are being grown for seed production. The larvae the bees produce in these "barns" are also harvested for sale to other customers.

The ability of bees to carry out pollination should not be under-estimated. The little critters are responsible for crops that include pumpkins, onions, cherries, oranges, grapefruits, avocados, almonds, and many others, and entire companies are devoted to selling bee barns where local bees can nest and thus enhance local pollination of crops and other flowering plants.

Bees have very sensitive eyesight, and unlike cows, can see colour. In fact, they have a broader range of colour vision than we do, and their sight takes them right up into the ultraviolet range where our eyes can't go.

On the rare occasion when a human exhibits the ability to see closer to this range, the condition is known as *aphakia*. It usually happens as the result of injury to the lens of the eye and sometimes also after cataract surgery. An interesting example is that of the noted artist Claude Monet, whose cataracts were so bad that he could only see reds and oranges, but when they were removed he found himself able to see deep purple and blue hues so vividly that they became an integral part of the colour palate in his paintings thereafter. You might wonder why the little bee barns out in the alfalfa fields are not red, but oddly enough, bees cannot see that particular colour, and though flowering plants of that hue are still visited by bees, they are often pollinated by hummingbirds. The plants themselves can become feral, as shown by the stands of wild alfalfa commonly seen along roadsides.

Resistance Is Useless

It's fair to say we've had considerable success when it comes to shaping the lives of barnyard creatures to suit our needs. But when it comes to the animals themselves, to what extent can they be said to have a will of their own? All domesticated animals retain certain inbred behaviors, to be sure, but often as not these constitute an inconvenience to the farm operator. Fear of predators, the urge to mate, territoriality, and the like can all be mitigated with relative ease. Keep the animals fed and watered and provide them with shelter and you have gone a long way to achieving stability. Other times we even harness some of these instincts for our own purposes and develop them for sport, as evidenced by such dubious pastimes as horse racing and greyhound racing, cock fighting and dog fighting.

One criterion considered of little importance for domestication is brain development. The suitability of an animal for mass production of meat and other products has little, if anything, to do with its intelligence. Breeders are not interested in making an animal smarter.

In fact, making it dumber is often preferable. This can have implications even for our own highly intelligent species, especially when it comes to things like the proliferation of social media. It could be argued that what such websites do better than anything amounts to a kind of domestication of the human species. There's no denying a certain aspect of the "herd mentality" pervades sites like Facebook and Twitter, where participation is as much about self-affirmation as it is about self-expression. A lot of what's going on has to do with compliance, with fitting into a particular paradigm of the social order, an algorithm of interaction designed and facilitated by corporate interests. Those who make the best candidates for inclusion exhibit an eagerness to "follow" or "like." What does posting or tweeting amount to but a "display," such as one creature might put to attract or impress or dominate another?

Then there is the whole aspect of grooming. We are nothing if not social creatures and, in that sense, no different than many animals, in particular the furry mammals with whom we share ninety percent of our DNA. Part of that deep-seated need for social interaction is a great fear of "missing out." The folks at Facebook and Twitter and Instagram are counting on it. Is it really surprising that the descendants of tribal creatures who like to hang around together literally nit-picking at each other should have developed social media? An even more cynical way of looking at it might be the extent to which are we being "groomed" by the keepers of social media for corporate "slaughter."

Are You Seeing This?

We sometimes see a depiction on television of an asteroid or comet, some lumbering boulder from outer space, as it comes crashing through the atmosphere in a ball of fire—the kind of thing that happened in the Yucatan Peninsula and wiped out all the dinosaurs. An animated version usually shows a brontosaurus or two munching on some swamp grass and gazing vaguely at the sky as the space rock hurtles toward Earth. The animals are invariably depicted as almost entirely without alarm. They see something in the sky, but it doesn't seem to faze them. A herd of cows standing out in a pasture during a total eclipse of the sun might simply start heading for the barn.

What does it mean for something not to make sense to an animal? Do animals even experience this cognitive process? The sight of a family dog cocking its head to one side at the sound of something strange is familiar to us. But what is really going on there? And how far down the chain of life does it go? Does the concept still hold up at the level of invertebrates? Is it possible to confuse a worm? Can an amoeba experience the equivalent of, "Man, I certainly wasn't expecting *that*!"

I Can't Take It Anymore

Do the large production operations constitute inhumane treatment of animals? Certainly animal rights activists think so, but to what extent do the creatures themselves "know" when they are being kept in deplorable conditions? The very fact that they are helpless to do anything about their confinement riles some people up. An idea has been seriously floated by animal rights activists that we should equip each and every chicken with a virtual reality helmet, so that it could at least be allowed the impression of living in a much better environment than the one it's in. Perhaps future barns could be laid out something like the holodeck on the starship *Enterprise*, a place where cows and pigs and sheep could be kept under the illusion that they are out on the open range, rambling around in the fresh air and freedom and grazing on virtual green grass.

We sometimes hear news stories of animals that have been starved or mistreated and it can be hard to watch. Does it ever occur to the animals to bring about their own end? There do appear to be instances of animal suicide, stories of cows and sheep jumping off cliffs in places like Turkey and Switzerland. When it comes to animals in the wild, there's that television footage of lemmings supposedly hurling themselves off a cliff, but it turns out to have been carefully staged.

Certainly there are recurring news stories about various species of whales that seem to intentionally beach themselves, but who knows what's really going on there?

When farm animals experience an excessive level of trauma, can they break down? There's increasing evidence that certain types of disorders may indeed be present. Depression seems to be one. Various types of self-harm or compulsive behaviours have been witnessed: excessive grooming, licking, scratching, biting, hair pulling. I once came across a chained-up dog that had gnawed a sizable hole in its own haunches. I called the animal welfare agency and the dog was subsequently removed from its owners.

CHAPTER ELEVEN

Raising a Stink

I may not know much, but I know chicken shit from chicken salad.
LYNDON B. JOHNSON

Get a Load Of …

Traditional barns have their share of detritus, the by-products of the wide variety of activities that take place there: old rope and baling twine and busted water hoses, rotted boards and rusted nails and wire. Burnt-out bulbs and broken milk stools and empty cans of spray, grain bags and salt lick boxes. Discarded water pumps and pulleys and pieces of steel and wood, splintered pitchfork handles and split shovels and wheelbarrows and stone boats. License plates, coils of cable and musty tarps, obsolete calendars, empty tins of salve and boxes of disinfectant. Derelict shotguns and worn-out knives, discarded boots and torn overalls, corn husks and slop pails, battered milk pails and leaky buckets.

There's also plenty of organic material left over, from milk and molted feathers, to straw and mouldy grain, to carcasses and offal and afterbirth. But without a doubt the most prominent of all is the copious amount of manure that accumulates daily in the barnyard. Cows in particular are big producers. A regular beef cow puts out about eighty pounds in any given day, but that dwarfs in comparison to a dairy cow, which plops down a staggering one hundred thirty pounds of the stuff every single day. Think about it, a single dairy cow produces enough excrement in one day to equal the weight of some adult humans. It poops about once every hour during the day, and if you do the math, that one dairy cow produces about fifty thousand pounds of dung every year, or about twenty-five tons.

It all adds up to a lot more than you might think. The total amount of animal waste from cattle and hog and poultry operations in North America amounts to about a hundred times more than the amount of human sewage produced every year. One large dairy operation with, say, three thousand cows produces as much waste material as a mid-sized city of half a million people. If the cattle are allowed to graze free-range there's not much of an issue. The manure is recycled right back into the soil and serves to grow more grass for the cows to eat. Neat and tidy, relatively speaking. But if it's an industrial operation, the manure is cleaned out, mixed with water, and temporarily stored in lagoons until it can be disposed of. Some operations employ an automatic flushing system that can use up to one hundred fifty gallons of water per day for each cow.

Whatever the means, it's not as if the stuff can be left where it falls for long, nor allowed to accumulate in any great a quantity. In some modern mega-barns the infrastructure includes an open-grid steel floor through which the manure is allowed to fall onto a network of scrapers and conveyors that carry it out to holding compounds where it will be recycled or pumped into a lagoon. But none of this existed in the big turkey barn my father built. The turkey shit that accumulated there on top of the plain dirt floor, layer by layer, inch by inch, stayed right where it was. The only thing we might do was to spread a layer of straw over it now and then to keep things from getting too messy. The straw kept the manure relatively dry and helped mitigate some of the odour and mess, but the build-up was relentless, until one day we'd be walking through the barn and notice that the ground beneath our feet had become quite spongy. By then the air was pungent with the smell of noxious chemicals whose concentration had risen to nearly intolerable levels.

The amount of ammonia produced by turkey manure, if not kept under control, can reach the point where burns and blisters began to form on the breasts and thighs. When levels approached 15 ppm, the respiratory system begins to fail. Exposure to excessive amounts can also lead to neurological problems that include swelling of the brain, impaired memory, shortened attention span, interrupted sleep patterns, inversion, as well as possible seizure and coma. And that's just in the turkeys.

And so the day would inevitably come when my father declared in his finest management-by-crisis style that it was critical, absolutely critical, for the barn to be cleaned out. The large sliding doors at either end were thrown open, as well as all the portals along both sides of the barn, to maximize ventilation for the job ahead. Feeders and watering troughs were temporarily removed, and as I deposited myself on the lumpy seat of the bulldozer to begin the work of getting all that rotting manure out of there, I prayed for a stiff breeze. I would start at one end of the barn and proceed to push the accumulated material out through the big doors, where a front-end loader would hoist it onto wagons and trucks to be hauled away for dumping or spreading as fertilizer.

Among the many tenets best adhered to in the barn is this one: the best kind of manure is undisturbed manure. No sooner had the blade of the dozer cut through the compost and exposed it, than the moist layers beneath released great quantities of foul-smelling odours and chemicals into the air. The stench soon became unbearable, and even with a good stiff breeze blowing in through the open doors of the barn it was difficult to breathe, and I choked on the caustic vapours that rose up.

Did I suffer any of the symptoms I mentioned earlier as I straddled the TD 9 International Harvester? It's hard for me to say. I was without question in a somewhat altered state of consciousness. Whether the thick column of black diesel fumes pouring out of the bulldozer mitigated or aggravated the effects of all that ammonia I can't say. I was in a fog. Mostly what I remember is choking, burning in the nose, nausea, and the general horridness of the entire experience—that, and being very glad when it was finally over. This was a familiar dynamic. So often the jobs I was compelled to undertake followed the same pattern: a long period of abject misery followed by a very short burst of unbridled euphoria when the ordeal was over at last.

On another occasion my father sent me into a granary full of fermenting grain, started the auger, and insisted that I keep it full until he shut it off. The noise and fumes inside the granary rivalled those of the turkey barn, and if I stopped shovelling even for a moment the metal innards of the auger began to rattle and shake with such a cacophony of urgency that I simply had to redouble my efforts in spite of my complete exhaustion—just to keep the damn machinery

Sketch of a Mennonite housebarn. It's traditional to have a row of small windows along the side of the barn to let sunlight in. AUTHOR SKETCH

from flying apart. And when at last my father shut the motor off, the sheer joy of my release from that hell gave my father an easy out. When I emerged from the bowels of the granary ebullient, nay effervescent with relief, he could tell himself that I was happy in my work and couldn't wait to do more of the same. He always did his best to oblige me.

In a traditional barn, things were different. The animal waste was removed daily, shovelled up out of the gutter and thrown into a wheelbarrow, then brought out to the manure pile somewhere in the vicinity of the barnyard. From there it would most likely be loaded onto a wagon and taken out to the fields to be spread over the soil. It made an excellent fertilizer because the manure of domesticated animals like sheep and cows and poultry contains high concentrations of nutrients essential for healthy plant growth. Such animals tend to have a digestive system that is not particularly efficient, so that the resulting waste retains a good deal of compostable material. Manure is still used today by many growers and seen as an invaluable ingredient in proper soil conservation.

Another Way to Go

We've seen that a single cow plops down quite a lot of manure in one day, in fact a single load is enough to generate about three kilowatt hours of electricity, which is about what you need to keep a light-bulb lit for the same period of time. It's estimated that converting the manure produced by all the cattle in North America into biogas would generate 100 billion kilowatt hours of electricity. To produce biogas, manure and other organic matter such as plant material and food waste are broken down into combustible gases which are then used as fuel. The practice has become quite popular, and more and more green energy programs include it as part of their overall strategy. It's considered a renewable resource because there's a never-ending supply of the stuff. One of the leading countries in the field is the United Kingdom, where biogas production is projected to account for as much as fifteen percent of all the fuel consumed by motor vehicles in the near future. In Sweden there are already buses and trains running on biogas, and thousands of vehicles across Europe run on the stuff.

The idea is even catching on in the movies. Bartertown, one of the settlements in the post-apocalyptic film, *Mad Max Beyond Thunderdome*, features a piggery that produces bio-gas to power not only the homes of the inhabitants, but also the vehicles that play such a prominent role in the movie. Other more ambitious and perhaps questionable projects include dumping animal waste into large, specially designed composting bins, then introducing large numbers of black soldier fly larvae for whom the resulting material becomes a source of food. The larvae gobble up the manure in prodigious amounts and grow fat and juicy until they get to the stage in their development where they are ready to undergo metamorphosis, the process that will turn them into adult flies. At this point their natural instincts compel them to begin searching for a suitable place to undergo their transformation. They climb up, looking for a way out of the composting bin, at which point they conveniently fall down into a row of feeding troughs arranged below, where they are eaten by the very animals whose excrement served as their source of food. The process is known as "self-harvesting," and the larvae are fed to other animals as well, including poultry, fish, and dogs.

There are other systems currently under development to recover not only the manure of these animals but also their urine, which is rich in nutrients as well. Cutting-edge projects are looking at urine management, including that produced by humans, as a growth industry. Organizations such as the Bill and Melinda Gates Foundation have designated a portion of their funds to go to research into the development of sanitation systems that recover the nutrients from urine.

A more traditional use for manure that's been ongoing for centuries is to employ it in caked and dried form as a fuel for cooking fires.

Primitive houses have long featured walls caked with cow dung as an insulator. In some parts of India they still mix it fresh with water and spray it onto the walls of their houses to act as an insect repellent. Early settlers liked to refer to the dried cow patties as cow chips, and in some places they still hold cow chip throwing contests. The record distance is 188 feet, 6 inches, set by Drew Russell of Beaver, Oklahoma in 2015.

My childhood friends and I recognized a number of variations in the nature of the cow pie. Those freshly deposited out in the pasture, shiny and perhaps still steaming and tinted a deep green, gave off a somewhat pungent but not entirely unpleasant aroma. In a day or two they had developed a thin brownish crust which if pierced exposed the still pudding-like verdant interior. These were ideal for prodding with sticks or shooting at with slingshots. There was no mistaking when the target had been hit, as the stone made a pleasing plopping sound and left a small crater. Dry cow pies were of less interest and chicken droppings were of no interest at all except as a source of amusement at the annual country fair, where an attraction still seen today was a regular feature: a well-fed chicken is placed in a cardboard box with a grid of numbered squares drawn onto the bottom of it. Gamblers place bets on which square the chicken will land its inevitable droppings on, at which point a winner is declared.

And the Winner Is

There are varying degrees of unpleasantness among the smells of barnyard waste but the nastiest by any measure is that produced by the pig. In some midsized cities in Canada and the u.s., one need only drive a few miles out into the countryside to find massive barns, row upon row, packed to bursting with hogs being raised for slaughter. Their proliferation has caused considerable friction between farmers and their nearby urban neighbours. In fact, the problem has gotten so bad that the u.s. Department of Agriculture has set up a Swine Odor and Manure Management Research Unit in Ames, Iowa.

Why does pig manure stink so much? To begin with, it's a complex cocktail of chemicals, a mixture of several hundred different gases and compounds, the most offensive among them being that old stand-by ammonia, but also hydrogen sulfide (the smell of rotten eggs). What really sets pig manure apart, though, is an ingredient known as cadaverine, which gives off the odour of rotting flesh. It's related to putrescine, both of which are produced by the breakdown of certain amino acids. These two play a major role in the foul odour of rotting flesh (as well as in bad breath). Cadaverine can be toxic to both animals and humans in sufficient doses, but, interestingly, it's not noxious to rats, which seem to rather like the smell of it. Modern-day hog waste can even be dangerous. The manure from massive hog operations is often stored as an effluent in nearby lagoons. Foam can build up on the surface and sometimes explodes. No one knows why.

It may also be that hog manure smells worse than it used to because the hog factories of today feed their animals a different diet than the one they got when I was the kid on the farm. In my day, we had a slop pail under the sink, and all the scraps from the kitchen went in there. When it was full, it was taken out to hogs and emptied it into the trough. The pigs went nuts for it.

Part of the reason we find pig manure particularly disgusting may stem from familiarity. Of all the domestic animals, the pig's excrement most closely resembles our own in composition. They have more or less the same dietary needs as humans, and the entire gastro-intestinal system of the pig bears a remarkable resemblance to ours. Stomach, spleen, bile duct system, small intestines, kidney, bladder, offer little to distinguish their species from ours. In fact, until very recently, medical students practised their surgical techniques on them. Their comparative anatomy and physiology make them excellent candidates for research in many fields of science and medicine. Because hogs and humans share so many similarities, some researchers are taking that ball and running with it, actively working to grow human organs inside pigs for the purposes of transplant.

Working up an Appetite

One day my father got it into his head that he would like to raise some pigs. His turkey operation was doing so well he had money left over to buy up other farms in other parts of the province. A lot of these places had been put up for sale by owners who couldn't make a go of it any longer. My father usually left the abandoned house and outbuildings empty and simply worked the land, but sometimes he would hire someone to run a little boutique farm operation for him. In this case, he had arranged for a couple to look after the place, a Mr. and Mrs. Fehr, with whom I would stay and be allowed to take my meals. The place had a large red barn in the finest traditions of such buildings. It had all the accessories and was about as close to picture perfect as any barn I can remember. At one time it would have been a place with contented cows mooing in their stalls, chicks pecking at the ground, hay in the loft—all of it. But now the barn was empty and my father was going to fill it with piglets.

I rode along with him in a grain truck one morning to fetch the young hogs from a breeder. He turned into a farmyard in an area of Manitoba I had never been to before, and there we proceeded to load two hundred little piglets into the grain box of the truck. Each one was about the size of a small terrier and the plan was to take them to the farm he'd just bought some hundred or so miles distant, pen them up in the empty (if idyllic) barn, feed and raise them to four hundred pounds, and then sell them to market for a tidy profit. The overhead was going to be low because there would be cheap labour (me) and because the barn was already there waiting to be put to good use.

The failing farmer my father had bought the place from had cleaned it out so that the concrete floor was spic and span when the squealing piglets were lowered onto it to run about in that rather clinical space. We inoculated each of them with a shot to stave off disease and also made sure their eye teeth wouldn't grow to full size (or they would shred each other's ears with them when they became full-blown fangs). In order to accomplish these goals a sort of tasking station was set up, a row of plywood tables where my father showed me how to perform a series of operations. I was to venture out into the crowd of piglets, get hold of one by stealth and guile, and bring it over to the waiting tables where I would force open its mouth, find the eyeteeth and crush them individually using a set of sturdy pliers. Next I would pick up a very sharp knife and, laying the now screaming piglet on its back, locate the small bulge near the back of its underbelly, slit it open and pop out the little gonad before neatly slicing it off. Twice. When I was done, I would grab a bottle of iodine and pour a little into each wound before releasing the little fellow into a separate pen, where it would stand trembling, trying its best to shiver away the pain of its emasculation.

I had only the most perfunctory appreciation for their trauma, as I was myself somewhat traumatized by the process I was carrying out, and in particular by the unearthly high-pitched squealing (it was really more like a scream) that accompanied it. It was so penetrating, so intense, that my only response was to try and make it stop. I remember that at one point I put my bloodied hands around the throat of one poor little piglet and tried to choke it into silence. How am I supposed to feel about that now? It brings me to tears. I was an instrument of torture. I think I understand a tiny bit about what sometimes happens in places like prisons and refugee camps and battlefields. I don't see how anyone could endure the horror of it for long.

Did my father, somewhere in another part of the farmyard, hear what was happening? Not likely. He usually had other projects on the go and he was "gone" almost all the time. I was on my own. But even if he had been there, would he have thought to come and see if I was managing all right? Would it have occurred to him that the particular son he had chosen for this job was the least suited for it? Perhaps he thought he knew me better by than I knew myself, and that he was making a man out of me.

By the time I was done, I was both exhausted and desensitized to the point where I didn't feel anything but tired. The experience inflicts a kind of blunt-force trauma on your psyche, renders it banal. How many times can you commit a stomach-churning act before some part of you shuts down, before the whole thing turns into something else, becomes an exercise in endurance, and obedience, and denial.

I have sometimes wondered if there have been any studies done to try and ascertain what the number is, the threshold at which a certain kind of cognitive entropy begins to insinuate itself into the mind of those committing of acts of brutality, or torture, or degradation. Granted, there are those cases where the psychotic may simply enjoy it, but I was never granted that luxury.

But I was getting around to the manure. Two hundred growing piglets produce a lot of it. As I said, the floor of the barn was concrete. The pigs were allowed to mill around and eat and shit, and it was my job to get the manure out of there every day. I was issued an aluminum shovel, the kind used for shovelling grain, and a wheelbarrow. There was a window on one side of the barn to throw the odorous muck out of. One entirely unexpected side effect of this job was that it gave me a tremendous appetite. It seemed to me everything Mrs. Fehr served up was delicious. I do think she was an excellent cook. The ham was especially good. I am not kidding about this. How am I supposed to connect the dots? Nothing like that happened when I worked with turkeys, or cows.

There was also a great bed to sleep in on the top floor of the house—which was a much nicer house than the one we lived in. It was cool up there, thanks to a big window, and a there was a lovely breeze. I ate the best and slept the best I could ever remember. I didn't understand it. In a confusing way I didn't want the shit-shovelling to end, but I had to go back to school.

CHAPTER TWELVE

Barnyard Lexicon

*I like a man who likes to see a fine barn
as well as a good tragedy.*
RALPH WALDO EMERSON

What a Load of …

"Bullshit," "horseshit," "chicken shit"—all slang terms whose origin traces back to the lexicon of the barnyard. Interestingly, "pig shit," the most repulsive of all, hasn't really developed into slang. It's hard to picture what "slinging a load of bullshit," in the literal sense, would look like, but the figurative connotations of this phrase are something we're all familiar with. Variations include "bull," "BS," "bullcrap," "bullfeathers," and others. The idea, roughly defined, is that someone has uttered something worthy of a dismissive response, and the word is often used as a comeback to indicate that the speaker has said something untrue, deceitful, etc.

Still, the distinction can be a subtle one. There are philosophical arguments out there that deal specifically with the delicate nuances which distinguish the connotation of "bullshit" from that of straight-up inaccuracy. Essentially, the "bullshitter" knows exactly what he's doing, knows precisely what the truth is, but deliberately sets out to mislead his listeners for the sake of some other agenda. This sounds a little like the idea of fake news, unless, of course, the use and propagation of that term itself amounts to a kind of "bullshit."

The "Bullshit Asymmetry Principle" was developed by Alberto Brandolini. It is sometimes known as "Brandolini's Law" and posits a variation on the law of diminishing returns. Roughly stated, it argues that the amount of energy needed to refute any given instance of bullshit is always greater than that needed to produce it. People in positions of power sometimes put this idea to good use, and I can think of one politician in particular who counts on this very law to sustain the endless absurdities and outright lies that spew from his mouth—not to mention his twitter feed.

"Horseshit" is a related term, but with a slight difference. Here the lack of truth is based less on deception and more on unfamiliarity with the facts. If you suspect an assertion to be untrue, and that the speaker *knows* it is untrue, you invoke "bullshit." But if you want to state that something is not true due in large part to the speaker's ignorance, you might utter "horseshit." In the case of a certain politician, the jury is out as to which is the more frequent practice. An individual can also be said to look like, or feel like, "horseshit," or possibly to smell like it, but this again would not apply to "bullshit." Something can also taste like "horseshit," but again, not bullshit. The term "horsefeathers" is a polite variation.

It isn't hard to fathom how calculated dishonesty came to be associated with something that comes out of a large ruminant's ass, but other terms aren't as easy to pin down. Consider the connotations for "chicken shit." It can refer to something petty or insignificant, as in, "How did I ever get into this chicken shit outfit?" as well as to a particular individual lacking in courage. The connection to cowardice isn't so hard to make, as the term "chicken" has been around for some time and since chickens tend to be rather easy to startle. The term, just like those others, is used in every level of society. Just recently, a senior official in the White House administration referred to a prominent foreign head of state as a "chicken shit." The Secretary of State quickly intervened to diffuse the situation, while the foreign media struggled with the possible subtleties inherent in the alleged insult.

When Pigs Fly

The barnyard serves as a well spring of rich euphemisms and aspersions. The term "gone to pot" originates in the idea of a barnyard animal that has outlived its usefulness and will soon be destined for the cooking stove. To "wake up with the chickens" is to rise very early. "A barn burner" refers to an exciting, often sport-related event. "Barnstorming" originated with travelling theatrical troupes who often gave their performances in barns. There are "holy cows" and "sacred cows." Someone can be said to "eat like a hog," "sweat like a hog," "grunt like a pig." They can be "greedy as a pig" or "dirty as a pig."

Men can be pigs, and back in the late sixties and early seventies some people referred to cops as pigs. George Harrison wrote a song back then about greedy capitalists titled "Piggies." Soldiers have been sent into battle "like pigs to the slaughter" and something highly unlikely will come to pass only "when pigs fly." Incidentally, an actual flying pig was a recurring character in a Canadian television sketch comedy series called *The Kids in the Hall*.

Barnyard clichés come to us from different origins, and in some cases it's relatively easy to connect the dots. "A roll in the hay," for example, is pretty self-explanatory, as is "Were you born in a barn?" and of course "Out behind the barn." Then there's "Closing the barn door after the horse is gone," and "He couldn't hit the broad side of a barn." There's even a unit of measurement used by physicists called a "barn" that is derived from this last saying and designates a fairly large area—by subatomic standards—of 10^{-24} square centimeters.

But what about something like "The chickens have come home to roost," an expression that's been around for almost a thousand years? "Roost" is a form of the word "rest." It origins are Middle English and it can also be used as a noun, the place where chickens hang out when they want to bed down for the night, i.e. a chicken roost, or a verb to denote the actual act of roosting. Someone can also be said the "rule the roost," often the male rooster in the literal sense, but figuratively an individual who dominates his or her fellow workers or associates. The original proverb itself may have stemmed from an association with someone suffering a curse. In the 1809 book, *The Curse of Kehama*, Robert Southey wrote, "Curses, like chickens, come home to roost." There's an element of Karma in the idea, namely that the consequences of an act eventually find their way back to the perpetrator(s) and lead to misfortune.

But what about the literal meaning? What does it mean to roost? Do chickens in fact engage in such a practice? And where exactly is home for a chicken? In the traditional barnyard chickens are kept in a coop from which they are allowed to venture during the daylight hours to forage about, and to which they return when darkness approaches. Once back inside, they seek out a place to perch, up off the ground, tuck in their necks and settle into a period of inactivity from which they emerge only when the sun is up again. A given chicken will choose the highest point in the chicken coop as the ideal place to roost. The main reason it wants to get up off the ground while in a relative state of inactivity is a general aversion to bedding down in its own poop. Chickens do quite a lot of pooping in their sleep and being off the ground makes it harder for parasites to invade their bodies. Also, they do not like to roost where they nest.

Another saying associated with chickens is the assertion that someone is, "Mad as a wet hen" which means they're really angry. It originates from a traditional farm practice meant to discourage brooding activity. When a chicken was allowed to lay a clutch of eggs it would sometimes go into "brood" mode, which means it became relatively inactive and chose instead to sit hour after hour on the nest it had fashioned and incubate the eggs undisturbed until they hatched into chicks. The hens sitting on these "clutches" would only leave the nest about once a day. To get a hen to give up its nesting behavior, some farmers employed a technique to shake it out of its inactive

Weathered boards along the side of an old barn AUTHOR SKETCH

state and get it back to producing eggs. The offending chicken was picked up out of the barren nest, taken it over to a trough filled with cold water and dunked in, then brought back up. The process was repeated until the hen had been shocked sufficiently into giving up its brooding ways. The hen naturally resented this abusive treatment and became extremely agitated and upset, which gave birth to the saying.

My boyhood companion would sometimes ask me along after his father had deployed him to venture forth and search out such nests in their barnyard, places where a hen might secretly have laid a "clutch" of her eggs, and collect them. The hens were amazingly adept at hiding their nests in out-of-the-way nooks and crannies, and when we did find them, they would be quite protective, pecking at our hands and flapping their wings to try and fend off the invasion. Sometimes, by the time we found the "brood," the eggs had been there long enough that when someone broke one open, instead of a pristine yellow yoke and clear albumen, a partially formed embryo plopped down into the pan that had to be scraped up and thrown out. And, yes, the poor mother hen would often stubbornly continue to sit on the empty nest well after the eggs had been collected.

To "Grab the bull by the horns" is a term that originated in the American West, where a cowboy would literally place both of his hands on a steer's horns and wrestle it to the ground for branding. It also played a role in perhaps the most effective advertising campaign ever devised to sell underwear. The ads were made for the Maidenform Bra Company and featured women engaged in various activities wearing only a bra above the waist. Some of the earlier ads had captions such as, "I dreamed I danced the Charleston in my Maidenform bra." Or "I dreamed I went skating in my Maidenform bra." But later ones became increasingly bolder as women made headway into traditionally male-dominated roles. Thus: "I dreamed I won the election in my Maidenform bra." And yes, "I dreamed I took the bull by the horns in my Maidenform bra."

The Horreum, the Horreum

There are any number of phobias associated with the barn including *doraphobia*, which is fear of the fur or hide of animals, *osmophobia* which is fear of smells or odours, and *seplophobia* which refers to an irrational fear of decaying matter. I was surprised to find the complete absence of a word for actual fear of barns themselves. Surely there must be people out there who break into a cold sweat at the mere sight of one. I mean, that thing with Tony Soprano was a bit of a phobia, don't you think? In the interest of science, I've decided to coin my own term for such a phenomenon. The Latin for barn is *horreum*, thus the term for an irrational and paralyzing fear of barns will hereafter be known as *horreuphobia*. And while I'm at it, as *faenileis* is the Latin for hayloft, *faenilephobia* will be fear of such places. And finally, *stabulophobia* will be fear of stables.

There is also some bizarre dysfunction associated with the relationship between barnyard animals and humans. *Boanthropy* is a disorder

The pioneer log barn, long since deserted, stands in stubborn defiance of its inevitable collapse. AUTHOR SKETCH

where someone believes himself to be a cow. People with *Totemism* believe they can turn themselves into animals.

Oh, Give Me a Home

Some terminology stems from a *lack* of barns, especially when it relates to the care of animals that lack shelter to take refuge in. Cowboys, for example, became necessary when the vast open ranges of North America provided plenty of space but not enough vegetation for large herds of cattle, which had to cover considerable distances in a given day in order to be able to graze enough acreage to keep fed. The cattlemen could hardly keep up with them on foot and took to mounting horses, and so the "cowboy," "cowpoke," "cowhand," or "cowpuncher" was born. A similar origin brought about the likes of the "drover," "stockman," "wrangler," the "vaquero" in Mexico and the "paniolo" in Hawaii.

CHAPTER THIRTEEN

Danger in the Barn

Make poor men's cattle break their necks;
Set fire on barns and hay-stacks in the night,
And bid the owners quench them with their tears.
SHAKESPEARE

The Next Thing I Know

For those who work in the barnyard, injury and death can often result from a machine or a tool that has inadvertently been turned into a lethal weapon. The many labour-saving devices that have been developed over the years also come with a dark side. One such machine is the combine, an enormous and complex apparatus used to collect the grain produced by the various crops at harvest time. It comes by its name honestly because it does three separate jobs all at once: reap, thresh, and winnow, i.e. cut and gather the stalks of grain up from the field (reap), extract the seeds from their husks (thresh), and separate the grain from the chaff (winnow). The forerunner of the combine was the threshing machine, a stand-alone operation run by a powerful steam tractor, to which the sheaves of grain were brought to be fed through. Early versions of the combine were pulled across the field by as many as twenty horses, and later gasoline and diesel tractors, but modern ones are self-propelled and a single machine operating at full capacity can do the work of thirty men. A new one will run you half a million dollars. Almost any exposed part of a combine can hurt you, whether it's the cutter bar or the grain conveyor, the auger or the straw chopper. Common mishaps are the result of getting cut, mangled, or crushed, slipping into the machinery, the combine tipping over, or just plain getting run over by the damn thing.

What is probably the most recognizable of farm machines, the tractor, is also a major culprit. These versatile implements come in all sizes and shapes, and modern farms employ models that are gargantuan in size and formidable in power. A new one will run you almost as much as a combine and can do just as much harm. The most dangerous part of the tractor is the PTO, or power take-off, a rotating steel shaft that attaches by means of a coupling to various pieces of farm machinery such as a baler, swather, and of course, the dreaded hammer mill. The PTO turns at very high speed and is often shielded, at least in part, but the exposed areas can cause a lot of damage if something gets caught up in it. If a piece of clothing catches on it, for example, it gets wrapped around the spinning shaft and you will quickly be pulled in.

As I'm writing this, I shudder to think how many times, in how many ways, I could have been killed or maimed for life by one of these machines. Indeed a number of my kin were injured or killed in farming accidents, and anyone with a farming background can tell a similar story. It could have happened when I stuck my hand into a piece of machinery (baler, combine, hammer mill) to unclog it. I could have tripped or got my clothing caught up in a spinning PTO shaft. I could have fallen off a tractor, been thrown from it, run over by it. I might have been struck by a piece of metal debris that flew off a piece of machinery. I did have my share of near misses, including a caterpillar track that became dislodged and whizzed by my head, also a steel combine pulley that did likewise. Then there were the times I narrowly avoided being crushed by an improperly secured payload, whether it was grain or lumber or barrels of gasoline.

I have traumatic memories of struggling to keep from slipping into the churning bowels of grain augers, and of jumping out of the way to avoid being crushed by various types of machinery, but I wasn't always so lucky. I've suffered injury after being struck by axes and shovels and hammers, stepped on sharp objects like nails and blades, had my feet and hands run over by tractors and trucks, fallen from roofs and ladders, and been thrown from the cab of a truck.

One mishap occurred when I was a mere toddler, riding in the cab of a grain truck driven by my mother. It was common practice at harvest time for a farm wife to prepare a meal for her husband to take out to him, and then drive back to the farmyard with a load of grain. I can remember how she would spread a blanket on the ground in the shade of the combine when she arrived, and how my father would come down off steps of the big machine to sit and eat his supper. I have no memory of the episode, but apparently on one such occasion, as my mother turned a corner on the way out to the field, the passenger door of the truck flew open and I was catapulted out into the ditch, where I landed relatively unscathed.

Unfortunately, stories abound of men and women and children who've had their limbs (usually one or both arms) ripped off by one piece of machinery or another. Other times injury and death are the result of grain suffocation, inhalation of deadly fumes, electrocution, chemical exposure, dynamite explosion, and heatstroke. In fact, farming is considered one of the most dangerous professions in the world. It beats out professions traditionally considered more hazardous, such as mining and construction.

Another dangerous machine on the farm is the hay baler. This unit is designed to pick up a windrow of hay or straw from the field and by means of compression arrange it into a tight bale wrapped in binder twine or plastic, after which it can be stored until such time as it is needed for other purposes, most often as feed for the livestock. The unit is pulled by a tractor and operates from a power take-off, so right there is a recipe for trouble. The danger exists when they get plugged up with hay, at which point you have to get off the tractor to try and rip the hay away from the problem area to free up the machinery. The bad accidents often happen when the operator fails to disengage the PTO and becomes entangled in the various moving parts. Victims often have one or both arms torn off. When the bales are ready, they are loaded on a wagon with a fork loader attached to the front of a tractor. Many accidents happen when these large round bales become dislodged and crush someone under their considerable weight.

The machine I feared most was the hammer mill, a powerful contrivance hooked up to the power take-off of a tractor and used to shred grain or anything else that needed milling. It consisted of a series of heavy iron blades whirling at very high speed inside a steel drum. The noise was deafening, and vibrations shook the ground. If a single one of the iron blades had ever become dislodged from the drum the centrifugal force would have sent it slicing through anything in its path, whether metal or wood or human flesh. The bowels of the hammer mill had two openings: one into which the grain or alfalfa was fed, and another which led to a chute from which the shredded fodder would be sprayed into a truck or mixer or whatever was parked under it.

As you fed alfalfa, for example, into the gaping maw of the hammer mill, the spinning machinery would grab it with such force that you had to be sure and let go quickly. You couldn't feed too much into the machine at one go or the RPM's would slow down to the point where the tractor began lugging and threatened to stall. It was a fine balance. Things happened. On one occasion a stray turkey that had wandered into yard somehow managed to get sucked into the thing and all that came out the other end a few seconds later was a red spray of ground meat. The grain auger was another dangerous machine. It consisted of a long steel shaft inside of which a spiral blade turned, driven by a small engine, so that when you shovelled grain into one end it was carried along until it reached the end and fell into the waiting truck or mixer. Here again a stray turkey might wander too close to the blades and get caught, at which point the auger would slow down somewhat as it tried to deal with the unexpected load. Usually just the legs of the big bird would be sheared off and come plopping out the far end a few seconds later while the bird bled out and had to be dealt with before you could get on with your shovelling.

Axe Me No Questions

I was involved in a farming accident in the very barn I would help dismantle only a year or so later. I've already mentioned that my father had a lot of ideas when it came to new and improved ways of running his turkey operation, and even though some of them turned out to be pretty good, there could also be spinoff effects that took things in an unexpected direction. In one such incident, it all began with solving the problem of how to feed twenty thousand turkeys in an efficient and practical manner. My father came up with the idea of building a whole series of large wooden containers he called "self-feeders." Each one was constructed out of two-by-fours and plywood (my father had a lot of ideas that involved plywood) and looked something like an oversized coffin, complete with a rounded lid. They were not only sturdy and spacious but portable, and could be pulled around the barn as needed. A gravity-fed trough ran along the bottom of each one on either side, and when the feeder had been filled with grain, the ravenous birds could simply gobble it up, assured that the supply would be continually replenished.

Naturally, there was a certain amount of spillage involved, which over time attracted its share of vermin. The plunder was so plentiful that if the feeder was left standing in one spot long enough, a large colony of rats would soon make their home underneath it. They would burrow through the mixture of soil and manure until they reached a feeder, then chew through the bottom of it, thereby gaining access to an endless supply of food. In fact, they were so well fed they became rather roly-poly and relatively easy to kill. We were encouraged to do this to cut down on the amount of feed going to waste. All my good friend Delbert (a fellow-rat stalker from the neighbouring farm) and I had to do was turn over one of the self-feeders when it was relatively empty (they were impossible to move when filled with grain) to reveal a labyrinth of burrows and tunnels beneath, not to mention any number of fat rats lying about sated and drowsy, who as soon as the light hit them, would do their best to scamper back into the tunnels they had so cleverly burrowed.

That was where our weaponry came in. I liked to use a heavy ball-peen hammer for the job, and Delbert preferred an axe. On one occasion, having thrown the hammer I'd been wielding at a big rat and only managing a glancing blow, I instinctively thrust my foot out to stomp on the stunned animal just as Delbert brought his axe down on the same target. The result was not a pretty sight. The blood spurting up out of my partially severed foot (the leather boot I had been wearing offered almost no protection at all) caused my friend to go into shock, and all he could do was stand there stupidly. This left me no choice but to take matters into my own hands. One of the hired hands had parked a pickup truck not too far away but he himself was nowhere in sight. I was years away from being old enough to get my driver's licence but that was neither here nor there. I was about to learn what a valuable asset desperation can be. If I wanted to get to the farmyard before I lost too much blood and passed out, I'd have to drive myself home.

The pickup was equipped with a three-speed manual transmission that would require me to engage the clutch on the floorboard and shift the gears if I wanted to get anywhere. The task was not made any easier considering that my partially severed left foot, still spurting blood and not responding properly to my commands, didn't want to cooperate. Somehow I made the trip back home. When I got to the house my mother (in a scene that might we'll have been taken from a Monty Python sketch) at first passed it off as little more than a flesh wound. This was in the days before universal health care. Upon closer inspection she agreed that I should be taken to the hospital, where I underwent a lengthy surgery, after which my foot was placed into a cast.

It was many weeks before I could have it removed but when the day finally came and I was free of the thing, I couldn't put any weight on the foot at all. The doctors were stumped until they took an x-ray and realized I had a dislocated ankle. It must have happened when I was working the pedals to make my way home in the pickup truck. They had unknowingly set my foot into the cast in that position, and it was going to be a bit of a mess to put things right. My mother got me out of there and straight to a chiropractor's, who taught me how to reset the ankle myself, should it come out again. I could be found doing so even during baseball games. In one instance I was rounding second on a ball I'd hit to deep right field, when, sure enough, the ankle went out. I sat down, promptly reset it, and continued on to third base while the ball was being thrown in from the outfield. I was safe.

This Is Gonna Sting a Little Bit

The barnyard can be a cruel place. It's understandable that George Orwell chose it for the setting of *Animal Farm*, his allegorical novella on political dysfunction. The drunken Mr. Jones is an incompetent farmer, and the unjust treatment of the animals in his care is clearly unacceptable. He doesn't give much thought to their well-being until his own is in jeopardy. The same might be said for a good number of real-life farming operations, past and present. While most owners offer humane treatment and supply good living conditions, some do not. Instances of cruelty to animals surface on a regular basis and become the topic of media attention—horses left to starve, poultry forced to live under horrific conditions, animals beaten and battered by their keepers.

There are also plenty of examples where pain and suffering have been deliberately inflicted on barnyard animals for what might be

considered more "noble" purposes. Cattle are branded for identifica-
tion, dehorned to prevent gorging, castrated so their hormones won't
slow their growth, etc. Chickens have their combs cut off (a process
known as dubbing), their wings clipped to keep them from flying
away, and their beaks severed to prevent pecking injuries. Turkey
chicks undergo a similar set of procedures for much the same reasons.
Adult male turkeys (called toms) will develop a beak with a raptor-like
hook on the end that's sharp enough to rip apart flesh. To pre-empt
them from using it on their fellow turkeys, the chicks undergo a procedure known as "debeaking" at a fairly young age. The top portion
of the beak (the part that would grow into a sharp pointed curve) is
simply sheared off.

The procedure used to be carried out with a sharp knife, but special equipment has been developed, and here again my father was
something of an early innovator. He modified a crude model of such
a device to make it more efficient and easier to operate. It made use
of a red-hot blade that accomplished the task in one pass with a combination of amputation and cauterization. When the time came for
debeaking I was invariably chosen to operate the machine. I suppose
I must have displayed an aptitude for it, perhaps a certain physical
dexterity, but it might only have been that no one else would do it.
It was not a job you would wish on anybody.

The young birds were herded up, caught by the legs, and brought
over to where I was standing before the machine. I would tuck the
terrified bird under one arm to keep it still, pry open the beak with
my index finger, and positioned the top portion under the blade.
With one foot on a spring-loaded pedal my father had designed, I
would bring the red-hot blade down and pass it through the beak. A
turkey's beak consists mainly of tough layers of keratin, and it took a
surprising amount of pressure on the pedal to force the blade through.

Each time the steel spring was stretched as I depressed the pedal,
it gave off a metallic groan, followed by the sizzle and hiss of the
blade burning its way through. A curl of rancid smoke went up that

smelled of burning hair and feathers. Sometimes my hand slipped or got bumped and the blade cut too deep, severing the blood vessels that ran along the upper portion of the beak and causing blood to spurt from the wound. The bird would wince noticeably when this happened and run off shaking its head from side to side after I'd dropped it to the ground. Did the birds experience pain and trauma? I have no doubt. Was I cognizant of the suffering I was inflicting upon them? Only to the degree that I was aware of my own.

One of the most striking aspects of the entire process for me is the realization that without exception, every single one of those birds resisted my attempt to force open its beak and hold it under that glowing guillotine. I cannot recall a single instance of a bird giving itself over to the process and simply allowing it to happen. And this is true for other creatures as well. There wasn't one time that a piglet passively reclined as the sharp knife I was using severed its testicles. There was inevitably a struggle. When creatures are made to suffer pain, they don't simply give themselves over to it. Why should we expect them to? The exception, of course, is us. We seem to be the only ones who can pull off a thing like that. Consider those Mennonite martyrs who are part of my ancestral history. Then again, perhaps it didn't happen just the way the history books tell it. Even Christ had a hard time. All that torture and suffering got to be too much for him in the end. He lost his composure for a moment and uttered, "Father, why hast thou forsaken me?" Can you blame him? He was only human after all, so where does that leave the rest of us?

Do the Math

The fact that many barnyard chores are monotonous and repetitive is the very thing that makes them dangerous. One wrong move with the debeaker, one slip, would have cost me a finger. And we are talking about thousands upon thousands of chances for exactly that to happen. Over the years I've had the opportunity to talk to victims of farming and industrial accidents and ask them about what happened. Their stories are strikingly similar. They were performing a task they'd carried out countless times before without incident, but this time, for reasons they couldn't articulate, they hadn't managed to get their fingers (or sometimes an entire limb), completely out of harm's way. Many of them expressed a mixture of sheepish surprise and mild annoyance that they had suffered such a terrible injury for no good reason they could think of.

I defied the odds, the law of averages—or is that idea based more on belief than actual mathematics? Roughly stated, the law of averages dictates that the more times I executed the debeaking action without incident, the greater the chance that eventually I'd bungle it. It's a variation on the idea that "what can go wrong will go wrong." Probability theorists will tell you this is bunk. They like to use the coin toss to explain why. Flip a coin, they say, and if it comes up heads ten times in a row, you have a strong sense that the next flip has *got* to be tails. Except the math doesn't support this conviction. In fact, the chances are still exactly 50/50. As comforting as it might be to imagine there was someone "up there" watching over me, I'm guessing it was simple math that kept me from searing my own finger off with that debeaker—same as it was for not having my arm mangled by the shaft a power take-off, or my hand ripped apart by the jaws of a hammermill, or my foot severed by an auger blade—you get the idea. Bless the probability theorists.

Size Matters

Adult turkey toms normally have a large bag-like appendage that hangs down the side of the head that's known as a snood. In a relaxed state, the snood appears flaccid and somewhat pale, but in a state of sexual arousal it becomes engorged, gets more rigid and longer, and turns a deep crimson. The most dominant males have the largest snoods, which become a target for rival toms when bloody battles for male dominance ensue. Combatants attempt to bludgeon each other with their powerful wings, scratch with their claws, and draw blood by pecking and tearing at an opponent's snood. To minimize the damage when this sort of thing happens, the snood is snipped off before it can grow too large. It looks like little more than a small bud on the top of the crown when the birds are young, so the bleeding is minimal.

Barnyard animals can and do inflict harm on each other. Left to their own devices, chickens will peck and scratch each other, pigs will bite, cattle will butt, etc. So it makes perfect sense, both humanely and economically, to carry out procedures that will keep them from hurting each other. But there's still the question of whether these behaviours might be more aberrant under other circumstances, and to what extent they arise from the way the animals are treated.

You're in My Space

There's a growing body of evidence that many of the problems associated with the care and well-being of domesticated animals can be attributed to manner in which they are kept. Normal behaviour tends to deteriorate when animals (humans are no exception) are crowded together in large numbers under artificial conditions. Desirable traits may be curtailed while more troublesome ones become exaggerated. For example, animals tend to turn on each other in crowded conditions with a degree of hostility otherwise found to be rare. Isolated incidents of pecking, biting, kicking, etc. become pervasive and sometimes lead to outright cannibalism. In smaller groups of birds, for example (say twenty-five or so) the pecking order of dominance and submission is easily established and maintained by means of things like posturing and feigned threats, but in a large flock the pressure to establish dominance can lead to violent attacks and actual wounds.

The propensity toward these kinds of behaviours appears to be inversely proportional to the number of turkeys or hogs or chickens in close proximity to one another. When housed under more humane conditions where crowding is minimized, procedures like debeaking become unnecessary, as problem pecking tends to disappear entirely.

In fact, beak trimming has already been phased out in some European countries including Switzerland and Germany.

Overcrowding also leads to the spread of disease, so that immunization often becomes necessary. Turkeys, for example, are routinely given needles to stave off everything from Erysipelas (bacterial infection) to Hemorrhagic Enteritis (a kind of Hepatitis) to Respiratory Disease Complex. Domesticated poultry in general are susceptible to more than a hundred different maladies. One of the unfortunate spinoffs from mass immunization is accidental injection of humans with these antibiotics or vaccines, sometimes resulting in serious complications or even death. A thirty-eight-year-old Nebraska man recently died after being accidentally injected with an antibiotic meant for cattle. A cow charged at him and in the ensuing collision an unknown amount of the vaccine was inadvertently injected into his body.

Fire!

Barn fires kill many thousands of animals every year. Modern-day methods of housing domesticated animals, whether poultry, hogs, or cows, employ the use of gigantic barns. A hog operation, for example, may have as many as five thousand hogs in one facility. When a hog barn burns—and they do so with disturbing regularity—it is a scene of horror and terrible loss of life. Barn fires are such a serious issue that in some places animal rights protestors regularly hold vigils for the animals that have been destroyed. Demonstrators lament that the creatures were essentially exploited as "non-human slaves" to the agricultural industry.

People on the other side of the issue argue that this sort of thinking stems from an excess of privilege on the part of the protestors. Bored, spoiled, city slickers they call them, fighting for a convenient cause on social media. Easily done, they argue, when the protestors themselves are putting nothing on the line, when there is no direct effect on them. But the effect on the farmer who lost his operation is very real, and often devastating.

Light My Fuse

I once set a barn on fire, an old log and plaster one where we kept all extra the stuff needed for the big turkey operation. The barn itself had no monetary value, but all that equipment in there was another matter. I had got hold of some firecrackers, the kind that look like little red sticks of dynamite and come with the wicks all woven together. You light one up and throw it somewhere. I was walking around the yard, doing exactly that, and when all the little fingerlings were gone, I went back into the house. Not long after, my mother was up at the kitchen counter as usual and remarked that there seemed to be something strange going on out at the old barn. Old cedar shingles were sliding off the barn roof and falling onto the ground.

I decided to go and have a look, and as I got nearer, I saw that this was indeed exactly what was happening. That was when I noticed they were also smoldering and realized I must have thrown a firecracker up there and set the barn roof on fire. It was going to be bad unless I got some water up there quick. To this day I don't know how I thought of it, but there was a black plastic hose running from the well in the yard past the old barn and out to the turkey enclosure beyond. I found a sawblade in the shop, cut the hose, and clenched it—water shooting out of the end—between my teeth. I scaled the side of the barn somehow (a feat I was never able to duplicate) until I was up to the roof, and doused the smoldering shingles. Back on the ground, I spliced the two ends of the hose together and my father was never the wiser. The whole episode remained a secret that my mother (who had witnessed it all from the kitchen window) kept with me.

Eaters of ….

Not a single traditional barnyard animal turns out to be carnivore. They're all vegetarian. Coincidence? For creatures in the wild, the interplay of predator and prey is the very engine that drives many ecosystems. The whole system functions on the premise of kill-or-be-killed, accompanied by plenty of pain and deprivation and merciless

People are still building working barns. This brand-new pole barn
will provide the young family with country-fresh eggs, home-grown meat,
and a stable for the horse. COURTESY DESMOND AND ALYSSA SCOTT

cruelty. Life for a predator is mostly long periods of hunger inter-
spersed with brief intervals of satiation. For the prey, it's a matter of
constant foraging, peppered with brief intervals of running for their
lives. The basic driving force of the barnyard is hunger, just as it is
in the wild. Everything revolves around getting fed. It's the reason
for the animal uprising against the negligent farmer Jones in *Animal
Farm*. The rebellion really only gets off the ground after the animals
have gone hungry.

Is it possible that all animals were once vegetarian? When did
they decide to start eating each other? I think it must have been early
on. After all, it's very efficient. You get far more bang for your buck
out of a chunk of flesh than a tuft of grass. Animals that eat plants
have to spend a lot of time chewing and swallowing and regurgitating
and digesting and pooping. Somewhere, sometime, the first animal

got the idea of eating another animal. Was it a strategy the creature thought up? Did it look over at a fellow creature, both of them grazing contentedly in the meadow, and think, "Hmmm ... this is taking up a lot of time and energy. I bet I can get what I need by just eating *him*!"

If predation is the best strategy of all, why haven't all animals evolved into meat eaters? But wait—then they would long ago have eaten each other into extinction. Some creationists insist that God didn't make any meat-eating animals, and that predation only came about as a result of the fall.

CHAPTER FOURTEEN

Good Barn Hunting

*Do not let a flattering woman coax and wheedle
and deceive you; she is after your barn.*
HESIOD

Barn Boulevardier

Whenever I find myself in the presence of a farmer eager to relate the many points of interest regarding the barn I've asked him to show me, I listen politely, biding my time until I can get up the nerve to ask the question that abruptly alters his expression and gives him reason to second-guess my motivation. It's not that I'm ungrateful for so much information, but what I really want most is the chance to *experience* the place. And so there inevitably comes that awkward moment when I pose the question.

"Would you mind," I utter with all the affability I can muster, "if I had a moment alone with your barn?" Awkward silence. But it's that intimacy I'm after. Those quiet moments that can't be shared with anyone else. For me there is something about being alone in a barn, *with* a barn.

One of my favourite pastimes is driving out into the countryside on a bright summer day to look for a barn to explore. There are an awful lot of them, and whether I'm on a country road in Manitoba or Ohio, it's never very long before I come across an interesting one.

It may be some distinctive feature that catches my eye, such as a particularly prominent cupola (it turned out to be a lookout tower!), an unusual addition being added (the place was being repurposed as a wedding barn), or one that boasts an unusual configuration of granaries and silos attached to it (a former brewery and winery run by monks). I turn into the yard hoping that the owner will make him or herself available so I can learn more about the barn. There's always some interesting detail of its construction or the history of its use or the disasters it has survived. There's a good chance one or more large dogs will greet my entrance into the yard with loud barks and much running around the vehicle. In such cases, I generally like to wait until the owner appears before I get out of the car. The dogs are invariably friendly and merely curious about my visit, but there's always that one chance …

Sometimes there's no one at home, or if there is, they're not coming out to greet me, in which case I turn the car around and head back out of the yard. It seems too much of an invasion of privacy to go gawking around in that situation. Sometimes I do go to the door and knock. On one such occasion my knocking brought two enormous dogs to the screen door, barking in a very loud and aggressive manner, which set me on my heels and about to retreat to the car, when a middle-aged woman came to the door and asked rather suspiciously what it was I wanted. I replied rather sheepishly that I had come to see her barn.

She immediately changed her demeanour and brightened up. By all means, she replied, go and have a look. Take as long as you like. I was glad to see that the dogs were going to remain with her. I made my way to the barn and discovered that it was completely open at one end, as part of a wall had been removed. There was plenty of light, and I became fascinated with the construction of the barn, which consisted of narrow boards laid flat, one on top of the other rather than end to end. It was then that I saw that the woman had decided to release the hounds, which were now in a dead run and headed straight

Looking out through the barn door AUTHOR WATERCOLOUR

toward me. One of the dogs was the size of a small bear and could easily overpower me. I prepared to be torn limb from limb but was merely subjected to some rigorous snout probing and crotch sniffing.

The woman followed behind and informed me that she and her husband were not the original owners. She couldn't really tell me much about the barn except to say it had once housed pigeons and that the oversized cupola had served as a lookout for spotting the birds flying about in the surrounding countryside. When she saw that I was genuinely interested, she became even more talkative, and I had to work to extricate myself from the place when it was time to go.

As I was saying, what I really enjoy most is the chance to *experience* a barn in quiet solitude. It's not unlike the kind of thing people used to do in big cities like London or Paris or New York. The idea was to have no particular agenda, rather to indulge in the atmosphere of the city, wander about in a state of heightened awareness that allowed the sights and sounds, tastes and smells to insinuate themselves into your consciousness: to saunter, to amble about, meander up and down the streets and alleyways with nothing much on your mind but what might turn up around the next corner. It was a popular pastime in nineteenth-century Paris, especially among those with a literary bent, so much so that a person who frequently engaged in the practice was referred to as a *flâneur*, or *boulevardier*.

I like to engage in something similar on a secluded beach. Saunter slowly along the shoreline with little purpose other than the hope of appreciating those aspects of the experience that might otherwise be lost to the senses. I apply the same principle as I make my way along a leafy sun-dappled forest path, or a winding mountain trail, or a peaceful country road. If I should happen to encounter someone else similarly engaged, a short exchange of words might ensue, but never long enough to break the mood of solitude both of us are there to enjoy. On the other hand, when I meet someone clearly intent on getting somewhere as fast as they can walk, a quick nod is best. Heaven knows I don't want to hold them up.

There are a surprising (and perhaps even disheartening) number of people out there for whom notion of taking *as much time as possible* to get someplace is an utterly foreign idea. They look at you in disbelief if you should make the mistake of trying to explain it to them. There is really just the one approach for them, and that is to get on with it. These two ideologies can clash just about anywhere, including the confines of a canoe. One of my favourite evening pastimes up at the cottage is to paddle far out onto to the smooth and glassy lake at sunset, meandering aimlessly in no particular direction before putting up my paddle to simply take in the gathering dusk, the lake, the birds in silent silhouette against a pastel sky, the world settling into summer slumber. But invite a friend to come along and the experience could turn out to be quite different. In one instance my companion was a very fit individual who insisted on taking the stern and snapped my neck back with each thrust of his paddle, leaving a small wake behind the canoe as he propelled us across the lake at speed.

And so it is for the barn. Any hope of discovering what perks the sighing timbers of its interior may offer turns on patience and long pauses and quiet reflection. It's not something you can rush. In fact, it's almost never a good idea to be in a hurry, whether searching for a memorable single malt scotch or the hidden soul of a barn or a city. One of the best days of my life is still the one I spent getting myself deliberately lost among the streets and canals of Venice. Bliss!

I Have a Theory … It Is Mine and Belongs to Me

While travelling through the small island country of Malta a few years ago I made a point of visiting some Megalithic archeological stone ruins carefully preserved there. They date back as far as 3600 BC and are among the oldest free-standing structures on Earth. There is no universal agreement as to what these ancient constructions may have been used for, or what their true purpose may have been. The general consensus is that they were temples of some kind, used for ancient worship, but I thought some of their features were not unlike those of a barn or stable, with nooks for sheep perhaps, and what might have been stalls for feeding and shelter. The ruins have no roof now, but did they once? Are they an ancient variation on the housebarn, albeit one used for special occasions and/or ritual sacrifice? I remember spending a long time in one of them, examining a crude sculpture carved in relief upon an ancient limestone slab. It shows what appears to be a cow, complete with a row of udders. I also found two bulls and a sow depicted at another site.

A very great deal of scholarly writing has been done on these sites concerning their nature and contents, and what it all means. Many of the sites contain artifacts of flint knives and the remains of animal bones. At Tarxien there are carvings of horned bulls. At Ġgantija, on the island of Gozo, they've discovered traces of red ochre paint. Others contain large stone balls and bowls that appear to have been used for grinding grain. In terms of historical context, considering that Neolithic farmers supposedly crossed the strait that separates

Interior of the Ġgantija temple ruins on the Mediterranean island of Gozo
AUTHOR PHOTO

Malta from Sicily about seven thousand years ago to inhabit the islands, it all adds up. Today about the only domesticated animals you find on Malta are sheep and rabbits. There's hardly an undomesticated creature to be found either, with the exception of a few shrews and lizards.

CHAPTER FIFTEEN

Bits and Pieces

Regard it just as desirable to build a chicken
house as to build a cathedral.
FRANK LLOYD WRIGHT

Sizing Things Up

One of the largest barns that ever existed was been built by Henry
David Watson near the town of Kearney, in Platte Valley, Nebraska.
It was constructed in the early 1900s and was so massive that nine
hundred tons of hay could be stored in the loft alone. It was three
hundred feet long, one hundred feet wide and fifty-six feet high. There
was room inside for three or four hundred cows, depending on the
account you read. It has long since been demolished.

An even larger large barn stood at the T. "Horseshoe" Smith
Ranch near Leader, Saskatchewan. It was built in 1914 and required
enough nails to fill up an entire wagon, plus half of a second one. (I
find this of particular interest when I remember all the nails we recycled for the big turkey barn, but I never kept track of the total amount.
There were a lot of pails!) It was four hundred feet long, one hundred
twenty-eight feet wide and sixty feet high. It was said the loft of this
barn could hold a whopping five thousand tons of hay. It could hold
seventeen hundred head of cattle plus an additional eight hundred

hogs. Thirty-two train car loads of lumber were hauled in to build it, as well as thirty thousand sacks of cement. It was taken down in 1920 and the lumber sold to help pay off the mortgage on the ranch.

As far as I've been able to ascertain, no barn claims to be the smallest in the world, but there are countless tiny barns to be found. John Ness of East St. Paul, Manitoba builds very small replicas of actual barns, expertly constructed recreations of the real thing that have been commissioned by their owners. He also builds toy model barns for children, and one of the things he is most surprised and pleased at is how much appeal these small buildings have for children and adults alike.

Longevity

The oldest extant barn in the world is probably the one at Cressing Temple in England, which dates back to the thirteenth century. It was built by the Knights Templar and still stands today. It was originally part of an extensive farming complex, and the funds generated by the operation served to finance various enterprises associated with the Crusades. The grounds included a bake house, a brewery, a dairy, numerous granaries, a blacksmith shop, various gardens, a dovecote, a watermill, a windmill, a chapel, and a cemetery. King Edward II turned the farm over to the Knights Hospitaller, soon to become the Knights of Malta, who remain sovereign subjects of international law to this day. Judging by the level of opulence I saw on display at the Grandmaster's Palace in the Maltese city of Valletta, I can attest to the fact that such farms harvested many good crops, as there seems to have been a lot of money to spend. The order still has its own flag (depicting St. John the Baptist, of course), as well as its own currency, known as the *scudo*, which the knights themselves mint.

Be Afraid, Be Very Afraid

A strong candidate for scariest barn may be the Barn of Doom located at Six Pines Haunted Attractions just outside my hometown of

Winnipeg, Manitoba. The place is so scary that people with pacemakers are forbidden entry, and it's not recommended for those who are pregnant or have a heart condition. Substantial numbers of people are unable to finish the tour every year. The site employs a cadre of actors who play various frightening roles from ghosts to ghouls to scary clowns and slaughterhouse employees. If you want the full treatment, get the "Hell Pass." If you don't want to be scared too badly, go for the "Chicken Pass." You can also ride through the attraction on something called the "Terror Train."

Or you can just stay home and check out the 1931 movie *The Haunted Barn*. It was restricted to viewers over the age of sixteen on the grounds that the sound effects of the wind howling in the film were too alarming for children.

Anything You Can Do, I Can Do

The most intelligent barns in the world may be those that have recently been converted into "smart barns." They come equipped with wireless sensors and monitors that control features such as temperature and lighting, and offer protection against power outages and vandalism. Cameras and monitors track individual cows and horses at breeding and birthing times to help their keepers stay on top of the latest developments in the barn. They also alert them to situations where intervention may be required, even if it's just that someone left the barn door open.

Yuk It Up

There's plenty of barnyard humour to be found, but a cut above the rest is the work of Gary Larson. His comic strip *The Far Side* often featured barnyard animals. He seemed to particularly enjoy depicting situations where the unsuspecting farmer catches the livestock engaging in some form of bizarre or unsettling behavior. In one strip, he enters the chicken coop only to find them in the throes of a full-blown egg fight. In another, he encounters a pair of cows busy drawing up a butcher's schematic of meat cuts, only the figure in outline is not bovine but distinctly human. In still another, all the chickens are dressed in mobster suits, and the caption has one of them bragging to his other goodfellas that it was he who "whacked" Old Macdonald. My personal favourite is the one where one of the milk cows has raised itself up on its hind legs, front hooves resting on its hips and udders exposed while it stares down at the farmer seated on his milk stool. "Man," the farmer mutters to himself, "it bugs me when they stand."

Occasionally it is the farmer who engages in aberrant behavior, like the one where Farmer Dan is seen whirling one of the sheep through the air in a circle because he has decided to give them all an "airplane ride." Other times wild animals enter into the equation, like the one in which a carload of hungry wolves can be seen crowded into the front seat of a bruised and battered vehicle, eyes bulging as their faces press against the windshield. They are approaching a sign along the side of the road that reads, "Sheep Crossing."

There are also jokes about barnyard accessories, such as the one where a psychiatrist advises his patient, a man who insists that his wife repeatedly mistakes him for a wheelbarrow, to stop letting himself get pushed him around.

Sexing the Barn

The barn is referred to in farmyard parlance as an "outbuilding," a term that encompasses everything but the house, and includes granaries, sheds, and stables. These are sometimes attached to a wall of the barn, which is without question the patriarch—or perhaps the term should be matriarch. In my experience barns are gender neutral for a lot of people, but when push comes to shove they are more likely to be referred to as female, just as is often the case with ships, locomotives, skyscrapers, and a lot of other things. It is without question the glue that holds the farm together and many an older farmer will grudgingly admit that he has probably spent a greater portion of his waking life in the barn than he has in the house.

I Found It in the Barn

Barns can be a place of discovery in more ways than one. You never know what you might find when you pull back the doors, especially if the place has been neglected for a long time. An old barn might be hiding something of real value, perhaps an overlooked item forgotten through the years. Stories abound of some lucky individual who explored an old barn only to dust off an item that turned out to be worth more than anyone could have imagined. Vintage automobiles are a popular discovery and have come to be known as "barn finds." One of the more noteworthy barn finds happened in the United Kingdom, where an extremely rare 1937 Bugatti Type 57S was discovered recently. The car sold at auction to a European collector for a little over four million u.s. dollars. A Tucker automobile worth three million dollars was found in an Ohio barn, and a blockbuster event in Portugal saw dozens of priceless vintage cars uncovered inside a single sealed barn.

Accounts relating the details of these exciting discoveries all have one thing in common: the barn doesn't get much press. The building itself tends to be treated as an afterthought, with the emphasis on the amazingly well-preserved automobile that was found inside. This seems a little ungrateful to me, considering the fact that if not for the sturdy old barn that offered protection so well for all those years there would have been no story. Searching out barn finds has become so popular lately that reality TV shows have sprung up, including an American one by the name of *Barn Hunters*.

If you should decide to leave the barnyard to venture a little further afield, you never know what you might find. I've come across things like a cleverly hidden crop of marijuana, a stunning fossil perfectly preserved on a half-buried piece of limestone, and an ancient stone hammer. Other intriguing surprises people have discovered include crop circles, artillery shells, stolen vehicles, crude oil bubbling up out of the ground, a volcano starting up, a bag of stolen cash, gold bars, a Roman helmet, drugs, mammoth skeletons, ancient weapons, early art, old coins, meteorites, arrowheads, Spanish doubloons, and on and on. Incidentally, the Roman helmet was auctioned off for 3.5 million dollars.

Run, Run, Run Away

When it comes to runaway farm animals, perhaps one of best known is Mollie, the young horse in George Orwell's classic *Animal Farm*. She's vain and materialistic and life on the farm doesn't hold much appeal for her. On the other hand, most farm animals seem relatively content, as long as they receive a minimum of care. Provide them with food, water, and shelter, and they will remain relatively docile. Unlike the caged wild animal we've all seen at the zoo—so restless in captivity that it beats a path along the perimeter of its enclosure, endlessly searching for a way out—barnyard animals lull their owners into a false sense of security. The urge to run wild has not been completely bred out of them, and given an opportunity to escape, some will jump at the chance.

A lot of the time the animals make their getaway on the way to the slaughterhouse. Sometimes these episodes become news stories that receive national or even international attention, especially when police or other authorities become involved. It might be a runaway cow causing havoc on the highway, a pig being cornered by dozens of police officers, or a rogue chicken disrupting the morning rush hour traffic. A disproportionate number seem to take place in the United Kingdom where they are often given catchy headlines in the newspapers like "Cow Causes Udder Chaos."

When it comes to animal slaughter there's a backlash developing against what is sometimes referred to as "big meat," which refers to the large slaughterhouses where much of the meat we eat comes from. Increasingly, there are smaller operations springing up, run by local butchers and meat shops, where people can inspect the live animal before making their purchase, and only after the transaction has been completed have it slaughtered and packaged up.

Two Philosophers Walk into a Barn

Barns can be a subject of discussion even in the staid and stolid corridors of modern analytical philosophy. In a notorious (at least in some philosophical circles) thought experiment credited to Alvin Goldman and Carl Ginet, the idea of a barn was used to explore one of the finer points of epistemology. This arm of philosophy (as opposed to logic or metaphysics) deals with ideas about what may properly be considered knowledge as opposed to mere belief. The experiment was designed to prove a salient point about the limitations of our individual perception. It imagines a young woman driving along a highway enjoying the scenery. As she travels down the road looking out of her car window, she admires a photogenic barn. But in fact the entire "countryside" has been ingeniously manufactured. In reality it consists of nothing more than a series of two-dimensional facades, including one painted to look like the front gable of a barn. So the barn is, in fact, not a barn at all. The "knowledge" (in this case ideas about supposedly real barns) she thinks herself to be acquiring is not true knowledge at all.

A precedent for this kind of thing may already have existed in rural Russia at the time of Catherine the Great. That case involved the construction of a fake village (neat and tidy) that had been set up in front the actual one (old and falling apart), a facade designed to give the false impression that the region was far more prosperous than was in fact the case. It became known as the Potemkin Village, after Grigory Potemkin, the governor of the region. He was a great admirer of the Russian empress and had been tasked with rebuilding the area after the terrible devastation brought on by armed conflict. Supposedly the mobile village was set up along the Dnieper River, and as Catherine passed by on her barge, Potemkin even had "extras" in place to populate the fake village, wave at the empress as she went by, then scurry into action as soon as she was out of sight to disassemble everything and reassemble it farther downstream for another showing.

The term "Potemkin village" subsequently came to be used in reference to any fabrication, literal or figurative, designed to give a false impression or to deceive. There are many instances of the "Potemkin effect" in history. To suppose there must have been at least a few "Potemkin barns" constructed for this elaborate ruse is not out of the question. My great-grandfather, Gerhardt Elias, grew up in a village not far from the banks of the Dnieper River. He emigrated to Canada in 1875 along with a boatload of other Mennonites from that region. No sooner had they arrived on the barren plains of southern Manitoba than they started up new villages modelled very much after the ones they had deserted in Russia. Today, if you wish to visit that village, you will not find it. Every last housebarn is gone. There's not a trace of anything left. When I stand out in the open countryside where the village is said to have stood, I try to imagine what the place might have looked like. The best I can come up with amounts to a kind of "Potemkin" effect.

A modern-day variation of a Potemkin village can be found in the DMZ of North Korea. Kijŏng-dong, a village in P'yŏnghwa-ri region, is supposedly a collective farm inhabited by two hundred or so local families. But according to local South Koreans who live on the other side of the border, the town is uninhabited, and there are weapons secretly in place behind the façade of the village houses and barns, complete with underground bunkers and military fortifications. The brightly painted buildings are merely empty shells with lights that come on and go off at pre-set times. Loudspeakers mounted on the façade of some buildings broadcast propaganda out to the South Korean side, urging residents to walk across the border and be received by the peaceful "villagers" with open arms.

Now Trending: Goat Yoga

"Animal yoga" is one of the latest fitness crazes to hit North America. The idea is to is bring your yoga mat down to the farm and lay it out in the barnyard. Seriously. Most of these places have a waiting list to sign up for classes. The mats are laid out and people carry out their various poses while ducks, chickens, pigs, and of course, goats roam about freely braying and mooing and clucking. They climb over and under and around the participants, sniffing and licking and rubbing their visitors. Do the downward dog long enough and a chicken may well decide to hop up on your back and try you out as a perch. The mats themselves can sometimes be casualties as well, so it's recommended you bring one that's not too pristine, since the goats and pigs and ducks scuttling about are likely to leave their droppings here and there.

"I got myself good and filthy," one participant was quoted as saying, "an alpaca took a crap on my yoga mat, but other than that I quite enjoyed it. Everybody has a different experience. Why not give it a shot, that's what I say."

When it comes to social media you can also find plenty of pics with people doing poses alongside various animals. You can even buy calendars that show cows doing different yoga poses.

The Virtual Barn

The British television series *Grand Designs* followed the ambitious design and construction of unconventional and ground-breaking homes. Along with architecture and planning, the hopes and dreams of the owners were an integral part of the show each week. Canadian Arthur Black narrated a weekly series for several years called *Weird Homes*, in which he visited eccentric and unusual houses people had built all over North America. There's never been a series on barns, but it seems to me these buildings can also be experienced vicariously in much the same way. How about a series called *Wacky Barns?* One that would surely qualify is at Miami-Dade Zoological Park and Gardens with that very name. "Wacky Barn" is a building of odd corners and crooked angles that houses a petting zoo. It resembles a barn put together by a drunken cadre of carpenters.

Or perhaps a television show could do for barns what the endless parade of cooking shows do for food. Would a show that makes barns look irresistible bring about an increase in folks who go out and visit them? The startling paradox of cooking shows is that not many viewers go to the trouble of preparing the recipes offered up. Studies show that people who spend as much as five hours per week watching television cooking shows only spend about four hours a week actually preparing their own food. Same goes for time spent looking at food preparation on social media and other online sites. Less than half of the people surveyed have ever actually tried to cook even one recipe they saw being prepared. Perhaps even more disturbing, of the viewers who *do* prepare one of the dishes, a substantial percentage admit to doing so for the sole purpose of photographing the finished product to share on social media.

The shows themselves throw up an ingenious ruse by making the preparation seem effortless. A host of "shortcuts" are used to give the television audience the impression of an invariably successful outcome. We don't see the outtakes where the sauce failed to thicken, the soufflé collapsed, or the chicken became stuck to the bottom of the pan. Stuff catches on fire, food gets dropped on the floor, people burn themselves. Guests screw up when they hand the chef the wrong ingredient or add too much or too little. In a technique known in the business as the "swap out," a dish just popped into the oven is exchanged during the commercial break for one already cooked. A dish that doesn't turn out well is swapped out for one previously prepared by a "behind-the-scenes" chef. There also are plenty of prop and food stylists on hand to make everything on the set look cleaner, more appetizing. The live studio audience has been thoroughly coached to perform like a collection of trained seals. A whole season of shows may be shot in a matter of days or weeks, and when people on the set take a break, they eat run-of-the-mill catered food. There are plenty of retakes, and if a dish calls for one rack of lamb you can bet there are four or five more on hand if needed for a re-do. And even after all of that, those amazing dishes the host tastes at the end of the show are often cold.

The variety of building materials used in different sections of this ancient Tuscan barn testify to centuries of repair and reconstruction. AUTHOR PHOTO

A Slippery Slope

When I was studying analytical philosophy in graduate school at the University of Manitoba, we spent endless hours working through the intricacies of what might constitute a set of necessary and sufficient conditions for any given proposition to be true. For example, we might have considered the stipulations that must be satisfied in order for something to be properly identified as a crow. The colour black would be a necessary condition, but certainly not a sufficient one, as plenty of other birds are black. Feathers would fall into this same category, as would a raucous call. But these three attributes combined would still be insufficient to qualify a creature as a crow. More would be needed to cross the threshold into bona fide crowness. Things got tricky in a hurry.

Now let's take this idea into the barnyard and try it with something like, say, a wheelbarrow. What are the necessary and sufficient conditions under which something qualifies to properly be classified under the heading of "wheelbarrow"? A set of handles would almost certainly be considered necessary, but far from sufficient. There would need to a wheel at the front, a box for storage, etc. At some point all the necessary conditions would combine to take things over the threshold into "sufficient." But wait. I have a wheelbarrow with *two* wheels in the front that works quite well, so an amendment would be in order. What if one of the handles breaks off the wheelbarrow? It still qualifies, doesn't it?

Now let's substitute "barn" for "wheelbarrow" and the fun really begins. Gable doors? Check. A hayloft? Check. Stalls for animals? Check. Have we got a barn yet? Hmmm. What about being red? A cupola? Is there something a barn absolutely *has* to have? I'm not sure. And what about the notion of the ideal barn? Can it exist? Can it even be conceived of? Maybe it's better to go in reverse. Suppose we do a thought experiment and imagine the perfect barn, that is to say, one that possesses every single qualifier for "barnness" you or anyone else can manage to come up with. Now let's begin to remove them one by one. Take away the loft—still a barn? Take away the gable doors—still a barn? The gambrel roof, the mangers, the rough-hewn beams, etc. A what point does the barn stop being a barn?

All of this is merely to illustrate that the notion of the barn—the truth about what a barn really is—may be a little more elusive than we might first have thought. Of course, none of this matters a whit on a practical level. Who but an addled and overworked analytical philosopher would bother with it? Even the most dull-witted, densest individual can lay claim to knowing what a bloody barn is and be perfectly capable of pointing one out. Anyone can conjure one up in their mind's eye without much trouble. And yet … Monty Python has fun with this idea in a song about Eric the Half-a-Bee that begins, "Can a bee be said to be, or not to be, an entire bee, when half the bee is not a bee …" William Carlos Williams liked to say that were "no ideas but in things."

Imagine the day when the last traditional barn is gone. It's entirely foreseeable that sometime in the future no such thing will exist, not even in a museum, when the last barn has fallen or been torn down, when not a single one can be found anywhere on the planet. Now let's take it a step further and suppose that all pictures of barns have been lost as well, all film, all visual representations of any kind, all references of any sort to them in literature, however abstruse or obscure. All gone. For all intents and purposes, it's as if such a thing as a barn never existed. Even the word "barn" itself has vanished from the lexicon. Lastly, all memory of such an edifice, all recollection has been erased from people's minds. We are talking *tabula rasa*—a slate wiped clean.

The question then becomes: could the idea of the barn still exist? Or would that have disappeared, too? Can the idea of the barn exist without some manifestation of an actual one, however tenuous? Does there have to be a barn someplace (even if it's only in one last lucky individual's memory) for the *idea* of the barn to exist? Is William Carlos Williams right? If so, is it possible that structures may have existed in our past which we have no idea about because all traces of them have been erased? Would we have any notion of dinosaurs if we hadn't come across the fossil remains? But wait. What about unicorns? And mermaids? And just how did we come up with the idea of a creator?

Right about now is probably a good time to end this philosophical workout, get out of the mental gymnasium, and head over to the local pub for a proper pint or two.

ACKNOWLEDGEMENTS

Thanks go out to all those who kindly granted permission for photographs and other material included in this book.

Also, to Gregg Shilliday, Mel Marginet, Catharina de Bakker, Sam K. MacKinnon, and everyone at Great Plains Publications.

And finally, to my wife, Brenda Sciberras, for all her love and support.